Celebrate with Mini Cakes

David and Charles

www.rucraft.co.uk

A DAVID & CHARLES BOOK

Copyright © David & Charles Limited 2010

David & Charles is an F+W Media Inc. company
4700 East Galbraith Road, Cincinnati, OH 45236

First published in the UK and US in 2010

Text and designs copyright © Lindy Smith 2010
Layout and photography copyright © David & Charles 2010

Content and images first published in *Celebrate with
a Cake*, *Storybook Cakes*, *Party Animal Cakes* and *Cakes
to Inspire and Desire*.

A catalogue record for this book is available from the
British Library.

ISBN-13: 978-0-7153-3783-7 paperback
ISBN-10: 0-7153-3783-1 paperback

Printed in China by RR Donnelley
for David & Charles
Brunel House, Newton Abbot, Devon

Publisher Alison Myer
Acquisitions Editor Jennifer Fox-Proverbs
Assistant Editor Jeni Hennah
Project Editor Beth Dymond
Designer Manager Sarah Clark
Designer Kevin Mansfield
Production Controller Kelly Smith
Pre-Press Natasha Jorden and Jodie Culpin

David & Charles publish high quality books on a wide
range of subjects. For more great book ideas visit:
www.rucraft.co.uk

Contents

Introduction

I love mini cakes; whether they are cute and adorable or bite-sized packages of sophistication. Making and decorating mini cakes is always fun, there is no pressure, you can experiment with design and colour and if you're not happy with the result it really doesn't matter – you can always have another go!

So what is a mini cake? For me it has to be a small cake, such as the 5cm (2in) round cakes used in this book, however from my students I've learnt that everyone's definition is different and many prefer the slightly larger 6cm (2½in) cakes or even up to a 10cm (4in) cake. I think the main aim of a mini cake is that it is personal, you make and decorate a mini cake to give to someone special to enjoy, rather than a cake to share with family and friends.

I made my first mini cakes quite a few years ago by cutting up much larger cakes. Today however we are spoilt, as purpose made multimini tins and shaped bakeware are now readily available, making baking and covering mini cakes so much easier.

These little cakes make superb mini gifts placed in small transparent boxes and tied up with bows or wrapped in cellophane with large and flamboyant ribbons. They also make a very popular alternative to a traditional wedding cake. Mini cakes can be tiered on special stands with a small cutting cake on top; once the top cake is cut the mini cakes are then distributed amongst the guests.

Have fun experimenting with my designs and don't be afraid of experimenting with your own. If you'd like to share your results, why not upload your images onto the Lindy's Cakes Facebook page!

Lindy

www.lindyscakes.co.uk

About the book

The book is divided into sections for the three styles of mini cake – Celebration, Designer and Children's – and within those sections you will find a diverse selection of small, inspirational designs. The intricate mini cakes can be made individually as exquisite gifts or in batches to give as favours at a wedding or to brighten up a special birthday or anniversary party.

Within the Celebration section (pages 22–51), you will find a wealth of impressive designs for every occasion. Glistening snowflakes are ideal for the festive party season, delicate pastel pink orchids are perfect for bridesmaids' favours, and the bold and elegant wine boxes would make a luxurious retirement gift.

The Designer section (pages 52–95) has incorporated a variety of traditional design themes such as those of Ancient Greece and India, as well as Op Art and Art Nouveau influences, for simply stylish results. You can also create musical notes, champagne bubbles, realistic flowers and delicate mosaic patterns.

The Children's section (pages 96–125) is packed full of fun, creative designs that will appeal to the young and the young-at-heart. Children will love helping you to create the prickly hedgehog covered in chocolate spikes, and the treasure chest and little mermaid designs are sure to appeal to their imaginations. The beautiful pastel baby blocks make sweet little gifts to celebrate a new arrival or a Christening.

Delicate jewellery decorates several mini cakes as crowns, bands or fountain-like toppers, and the book also describes how to develop the style even further for your own creations. Various decorative techniques are included, as well as a miscellany of effects you can achieve with cut-out shapes and textures. Full step-by-step carving descriptions and templates for decorations mean that even those designs that seem the most complex are broken down into clearly explained stages.

How to use this book

Read the reference section at the front of the book thoroughly. It explains how to begin tackling the cakes as well as some basic techniques. The projects use a variety of implements, and the most frequently used are listed in the Equipment List on pages 10–11. Where particular makes of cutters or decorations are specified in the projects you will find an abbreviation for the name of the supplier in brackets. Please refer to the abbreviations list with Suppliers on page 126.

Recipes for the cakes, including baking times and ingredients lists, as well as all the different types of icing and sugar glue used in the book, are provided. To help you create the cakes, a few templates are provided alongside the text.

For a professional look you will need to use paste colours and dusts. These can be obtained from cake-decorating stores or by mail order. Suppliers of equipment and ingredients can be found at the back of the book.

Some of the images used in this book show how techniques are used on larger cakes. Please note that these are for reference and, although the sizing will be different, the techniques will be exactly the same for mini cakes.

Tackling Cakes

Although you will be keen to get started, take a little time to read this section so that you are familiar with some important and basic points.

Preparation & time planning

Before you start your chosen project, read through the instructions carefully so that you understand what is involved and how much time to allow. Make sure you have all the materials and items of equipment to hand to complete the project.

Try not to leave everything to the last minute, and plan your decorating time in advance. As the cakes baked from the recipes in this book last about two weeks, you have about one week to decorate the cakes, leaving a week for them to be eaten.

If your cakes are to be creations that you will be proud of, you will need to be fully prepared.

Lining tins

Small standard cake tins

1 Measure the circumference of your tin and cut a strip of baking parchment slightly longer to allow for an overlap. Make the strip 5cm (2in) deeper than the height of the tin. Fold up 2.5cm (1in) along the bottom of the strip. For a round or heart-shaped tin cut this fold with diagonal cuts. For a square, rectangular or hexagonal tin, crease the strip at intervals equal to the length of the inside edges of the tin, and then cut the folded section where it is creased into mitres (**A**).

2 Grease the tin and place the strip around the side(s) with the cut edge on the base. Position baking parchment to fit the base (**B**).

Multimini tins

Cut a square of baking parchment to fit the base of the tray. Position the baking rings/shapes in place on top. Cut strips of baking parchment slightly higher than the sides of each mini cake mould and place inside each one; there is no need to fold and cut one edge.

Shaped tins

Grease the tins well then sprinkle on some flour, shake the flour to cover all the greased surfaces and remove the excess. Alternatively there are a number of products designed specifically to prevent cakes sticking in tins. Some are brushed on whereas others are sprayed.

Levelling the cake

Making an accurate cake base is an important part of creating your little masterpieces. There are commercial cake levellers available, but I find I get the best results by using a knife and the top edge of the tin the cake was baked in.

 tip   *Mini cakes can dry out quickly so try not to leave them uncovered for any length of time.*

Freezing & carving cakes

Some of the projects require the mini cakes to be frozen. This allows you not only to bake the cakes in advance but also to carve more intricate shapes without the cakes crumbling and falling apart. The interesting cone shaped cake in Rustic Leaves (pages 84–89) for example, would crumble during carving if the cake was unfrozen, and the rounded shape would be harder to achieve. How hard your cake freezes will depend on your freezer's settings so it may be necessary to let it defrost slightly before attempting to carve.

To cut cakes into different shapes, use a sharp serrated knife and carve off a little at a time until the required shape is achieved. If you remove more than you intended, remedial action can be taken by sticking pieces of cake on again using a little buttercream.

Ready-made decorations

There is an ever-increasing variety of ready-made decorations available from supermarkets and sugarcraft suppliers, and, used wisely, they are a great way of saving time and adding that extra touch. I particularly like the sugar balls that I have used on a number of projects in this book, as they add a touch of glamour and opulence to the cakes, such as the tiled roof on the Fairytale Castle (pages 122–125).

Storage

Protect your mini cakes by placing them in a clean, covered cake box and store somewhere cool and dry, but never in a refrigerator. If the box is slightly larger than the cakes and they are to be transported, use non-slip matting to prevent them from moving. Modelling-paste models can be kept forever if placed in a dry, sealed case and stored in the dark. They make a wonderful memento of a special occasion.

The following conditions will affect your decorated cake:

- Sunlight will fade and alter the colours of icing, so always store in a dark place.
- Humidity can have a disastrous effect on decorations, causing the icing to become soft and models to droop.
- Heat can melt icing, especially buttercream.

Equipment List

The following is a list of equipment that have been frequently used for the projects in this book. Details can be obtained from the Suppliers list on page 126.

Cake boards:
- Drum, a thick board to display cakes (**1**)
- Hardboard, a thin strong board used in the construction of stacked cakes (**2**)

Cocktail stick (toothpick), used as a marker and to transfer small amounts of paste colour (**3**)

Cutters come in various shapes and sizes for cutting out and embossing shapes (**4**)

Dowels are used to support tiered cakes and make them stable (**5**)

Foam pad (PME), creates a surface on which to thin flower petals (**6**)

Measuring spoons for accurate measurement of ingredients (**7**)

Moulds, daisy centre stamps (JEM) used for creating flower centres (**8**)

Multi-ribbon cutter (FMM) a time-saving tool for cutting strips of paste (**9**)

Oasis fix, a florist's adhesive for securing wires inside the posy pick (**10**)

Paintbrushes for stippling, painting and dusting (**11**)

Paint palette for mixing paste colours and dusts prior to painting (**12**)

Palette knife for cutting paste (**13**)

Pins (glass-headed dressmakers') to hold templates temporarily in position (**14**)

Piping tubes (tips) used for piping royal icing and cutting out small circles (**15**)

Posy pick for inserting onto cakes to hold wires (**16**)

Reusable piping bag and coupler to hold royal icing for piping (**17**)

Rolling pin for rolling out different types of paste (**18**)

Scissors for cutting templates and trimming paste to shape (**19**)

Set square for accurate alignment (**20**)

Smoother helps to create a smooth and even finish to sugarpaste (rolled fondant) (**21**)

Spacers, narrow and 5mm (³⁄₁₆in), for rolling out paste (**22**)

Spirit level to check dowels are vertical and tops of cakes are horizontal (**23**)

Stick embossers (HP), small embosser used to add patterns to paste (**24**)

Sugar shaper and discs to create pieces of uniformly shaped modelling paste (**25**)

Tins (pans) (AS), small ball, multisized square and 5cm (2in) multiminis, for baking cakes (**26**)

Tools:
- **Ball tool** (FMM) gives even indentations in paste and softens the edges of petals (**27**)
- **Dresden tool** (FMM) to create marking on paste (**28**)
- **Cutting wheel** (PME) to use instead of a knife to avoid dragging the paste (**29**)
- **Scriber** (PME) for scribing around templates (**30**)
- **Craft knife** for intricate cutting tasks (**31**)
- **Quilting tool** (PME) for adding stitching lines (**32**)
- **Fluting tool** (JEM) for creating open centres in cut-out shapes (**33**)

Work board, non-stick, used for rolling out pastes (**34**)

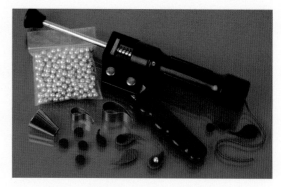

Using the correct equipment will ensure professional results quickly and simply.

Piping tubes

The following piping tubes (tips) have been used in the book. As tube numbers vary with different suppliers, always check the tube diameter:

Tube No. (PME)	Diameter
1	1mm (1/32in)
1.5	1.2mm (1/32in)
2	1.5mm (1/16in)
4	3mm (3/32in)
16	5mm (3/16in)
17	6mm (1/4in)
18	7mm (9/32in)

Cup and US measurements

For readers who prefer to use cup measurements, please use the following conversions (note: 1 tbsp = 15ml; Australian tablespoons are 20ml):

butter 100g (3½oz) = 1 stick, 225g (8oz) = 1 cup, 25g (1oz) = 2 tbsp, 15g (½oz) = 1 tbsp

caster (superfine) sugar 200g (7oz) = 1 cup, 25g (1oz) = 2 tbsp

desiccated (dry unsweetened shredded) coconut 75g (3oz) = 1 cup, 4 tbsp = 25g (1oz)

flour 150g (5oz) = 1 cup

glacé (candied) cherries 225g (8oz) = 1 cup

icing (confectioners') sugar 115g (4oz) = 1 cup

liquid 250ml (9fl oz) = 1 cup, 125ml (4fl oz) = ½ cup

soft brown sugar 115g (4oz) = 1 cup

sultanas 175g (6oz) = 1 cup

Baking Cakes

The projects in this book have been made using tried-and-tested recipes for Madeira, chocolate and fruit cake, which will give you perfect results.

Madeira cake

A firm, moist cake, Madeira will keep for up to two weeks. Allow one week to decorate it and one for it to be eaten.

The following will make enough batter for using the 5cm (2in) round multimini cake pans, an 18cm (7in) round cake or a 15cm (6in) square cake:

- **Unsalted butter (sweet butter)**: 225g (8oz)
- **Caster sugar (superfine sugar)**: 225g (8oz)
- **Self-raising flour (self-rising flour)**: 225g (8oz)
- **Plain flour (all-purpose flour)**: 115g (4oz)
- **Eggs (large) (US extra large)**: 4

Baking time at 160°C/325°F/Gas 3: 1–1¼ hours

1 Preheat the oven to 160°C/325°F/Gas 3. Grease and line the cake tin (pan) with baking parchment (see page 8).

2 Cream the butter and sugar in a large mixing bowl until light, fluffy and pale. Sift the flours together in a separate bowl.

3 Beat the eggs into the creamed mixture, one at a time, following each with a spoonful of flour, to prevent the mixture curdling.

tip *For useful tips, read the Lindy's Cakes blog article on 'Baking the Perfect Madeira Cake'.*

4 Sift the remaining flour into the creamed mixture and fold in carefully with a large metal spoon. Add the flavouring, if using (see below).

5 Transfer to the lined bakeware and bake for the time given. Baking times will depend on your oven, the cake tin used and the depth of the cake. When the cake is ready it will be well risen, firm to the touch and a skewer inserted into the centre will come out clean.

6 Leave the cake to cool in the tin then, leaving the lining paper on, wrap the cake in foil or place in an airtight container for at least 12 hours before cutting, to allow the cake to settle.

Flavourings

Traditionally, Madeira cake was flavoured with lemon, but it can also be made with other flavourings (flavourings are given for the recipe above; increase or decrease the amounts for other quantities):

- **Lemon**: Grated rind of 1½ lemons
- **Vanilla**: 3.5ml (¾ tsp) vanilla extract
- **Cherry**: 225g (8oz) glacé (candied) cherries, halved
- **Fruit**: 225g (8oz) sultanas (golden raisins), currants, raisins or dates
- **Coconut**: 70g (3¾oz) desiccated (dry unsweetened shredded) coconut
- **Almond**: 3.5ml (¾ tsp) almond extract and 30ml (2 tbsp) ground almonds

Chocolate cake

This is a rich, moist, yet firm, chocolate cake. The secret to success is to use good-quality chocolate with a reasonably high cocoa solids content; chocolate with a cocoa solids content of around 50 per cent or higher works well.

The following will make enough batter for using the 5cm (2in) round multimini cake pans, an 18cm (7in) round cake or a 15cm (6in) square cake:

- **Plain chocolate (semi-sweet chocolate)**: 225g (8oz)
- **Unsalted butter (sweet butter)**: 175g (6oz)
- **Caster sugar (superfine sugar)**: 175g (6oz)
- **Self-raising flour (self-rising flour)**: 175g (6oz)
- **Icing sugar (confectioner's sugar)**: 40g (1½oz)
- **Eggs (large) (US extra large)**: 6

Baking time at 160°C/325°F/Gas 3: 1–1¼hours

1 Preheat the oven to 180°C/350°F/Gas 4. Grease and line the cake tin (pan) with baking parchment (see page 8).

2 Melt the chocolate, either in a heatproof bowl over a pan of simmering water or in a microwave. Cream the butter and sugar in a large mixing bowl until light, fluffy and pale.

tip Carefully break each egg into a cup to prevent small pieces of eggshell falling into the batter.

3 Separate the eggs. Gradually add the egg yolks, then the melted chocolate to the creamed mixture. In a separate bowl, whisk the egg whites until they form soft peaks. Gradually whisk the icing sugar into the egg whites.

4 Sift the flour into another bowl and, using a large metal spoon, fold the flour alternately with the egg whites into the chocolate and egg mixture.

5 Transfer the mixture into the lined bakeware, and bake. Baking times will depend on your oven, the cake tin used and the depth of the cake. Check small cakes after 30 minutes, medium-sized cakes after an hour, and large cakes after 2 hours. When the cake is baked it will be well risen, firm to the touch and a skewer inserted into the centre will come out clean.

6 Allow the cake to cool completely in the tin, then, leaving the lining paper on, wrap the cake in foil or place in an airtight container for at least 12 hours before cutting to allow the cake to settle.

Make small batches of different cake flavours to cater for all tastes.

Fruit cake

Fruit cake should be aged for at least one month to allow the flavour to mature. Wedding cakes are traditionally stored for at least three months to give them a nicely matured flavour and to enable the cake to be cut cleanly into small portions.

The following will make enough batter for using the 5cm (2in) round multimini cake pans, an 18cm (7in) round cake or a 15cm (6in) square cake:

- **Sultanas (golden raisins)**: 175g (6oz)
- **Currants**: 175g (6oz)
- **Raisins**: 175g (6oz)
- **Chopped peel**: 75g (3oz)
- **Brandy**: 25ml (1½ tbsp)
- **Plain (all-purpose) flour**: 175g (6oz)
- **Ground almonds**: 40g (1½oz)
- **Mixed spice**: 3.5ml (¾ tsp)
- **Butter**: 175g (6oz)
- **Soft brown sugar**: 175g (6oz)
- **Eggs (large) (US extra large)**: 3
- **Black treacle (molasses)**: 15ml (1 tbsp)
- **Vanilla extract**: 2.5ml (½ tsp)
- **Glace (candied) cherries**: 75g (3oz)
- **Chopped almonds**: 40g (1½oz)
- **Lemon rind and juice**: ¾

Baking time at 150°C/300°F/Gas 2: 1 hour
Baking time at 120°C/250°F/Gas ½: 2¼ hours

1 Soak the sultanas, currants, raisins and chopped peel in brandy overnight.

2 Preheat the oven to 150°C/300°F/Gas 2. Sieve the flour, ground almonds and spice into a bowl. In another bowl cream the butter and sugar until light, fluffy and pale. Do not overbeat.

 tip For more useful tips visit the Lindy's Cakes blog article on 'Baking Mini Fruit Cakes'.

3 Lightly mix together the eggs, treacle and vanilla. Beat into the creamed mixture a little at a time adding a spoonful of flour after each addition.

4 Rinse the cherries and chop. Add to the fruit with the chopped almonds, lemon rind and juice, and a small amount of flour. Fold the remaining flour into the creamed mixture, followed by the dried fruit. Add extra brandy or milk if necessary.

5 Spoon into a lined cake tin (pan), level the top, and then slightly hollow the centre. Tie a double layer of brown paper or newspaper around the outside of the tin to protect the cake during cooking, and place a container of water in the oven to help keep your cake moist.

6 Bake for the stated cooking time and then reduce the temperature to 120°C/250°F/Gas ½ and bake further for the time suggested. When the cake is baked it will be firm to the touch and a skewer inserted into the centre will come out clean. Allow the cake to cool in the tin. You can add extra brandy to the cake while it is still cooling if you like. Prick the surface all over with a skewer and spoon some brandy over: 7.5ml (1½ tsp) for small cakes, 15ml (1 tbsp) for a 20cm (8in) cake increasing to 30ml (2 tbsp) for the larger cakes.

7 Leaving the lining paper on, wrap the cake in baking parchment and then foil. Never store your cake in foil only, as the acid in the fruit will attack the foil. Store the cake in a cool, dry place.

Mini Cakes

These delightful bitesize and mini cakes are great fun to make and are ideal to give as presents. An ever-growing selection of bakeware is available that allows you to bake a number of small cakes at once

Creating mini cakes

1 Choose a recipe for your mini cakes – each of the recipes on pages 12–14 work well – and preheat your oven. To prevent the cakes sticking to the tins (pans) either line or grease the tins as detailed on page 8.

2 Make the cake batter following the recipe; the amount of mixture you will require will depend on the size and number of the cakes you are baking.

3 Half-fill each section of the cake tin with the mixture (**A**) and bake; the time required will depend on the size of the cakes, but as a guide shaped mini cake tins usually take 15–20 minutes, bitesize mini cakes take 7–10 minutes and a batch of multimini cake tins take slightly less time than a whole cake of a similar size. Leave the cakes to cool in the tin.

4 Level the cakes by taking a large knife and carving across the top of each cake, using the edge of the tin as a guide (**B**). Place the cakes on waxed paper with the shaped side uppermost, and cover with a thin layer of buttercream.

5 Roll some sugarpaste (rolled fondant) to a depth of 5mm (³⁄₁₆in). Lift the paste over the top of one cake. Smooth the surface of the cake to remove any lumps and bumps. Then take a smoother and, while pressing down, run the flat edge around the base of the cake to create a clean cutting line (**C**). Trim away the excess paste with a palette knife. Repeat for the remaining cakes.

6 Once the sugarpaste has dried, decorate as you like; for example, using thinly rolled modelling paste cut into shapes using cutters (**D**).

Appealing and fun mini cakes can be quite simple to make, such as these cheerful giraffes.

Covering Cakes & Boards

Achieving the smoothest covering for your cake and board will give your cake a neat and professional appearance. With care and practice you will soon find that you have the perfect covering for decorating.

Covering a cake with marzipan

A fruit cake should be covered with marzipan before the sugarpaste (rolled fondant) covering is applied, to add flavour, to seal in the moisture and to prevent the fruit in the cake staining the sugarpaste.

1 Unwrap the cake and roll over the top with a rolling pin to flatten it slightly. If the cake is to sit on a silver-covered cake board cover the top of the cake with a very thin layer of marzipan and then roll over this with a rolling pin (**A**). (The cake will be inverted, and this is to prevent the acid in the fruit dissolving the silver covering of the board – especially important if the cake is going to be kept for any length of time once covered.)

2 Turn the cake over so that the flatter surface (the base) becomes the top, and place on a piece of waxed paper.

3 Knead the marzipan so that it becomes supple; do not over-knead as this releases oils from the marzipan and changes its consistency.

4 Brush warm apricot glaze into the gap around the base of the cake. Roll a long sausage of marzipan and place it around the base of the cake. Press it under the cake with the help of a smoother, to fill any gaps (**B**).

5 Brush the cake with warm apricot glaze to help stick the marzipan and use small pieces of marzipan to fill any holes in the cake for an even surface. Roll out the marzipan between 5mm (³⁄₁₆in) spacers, using icing (confectioners') sugar or white vegetable fat (shortening) to stop it sticking to your work board or work surface. Turn the marzipan around while rolling to maintain an appropriate shape, but do not turn the marzipan over.

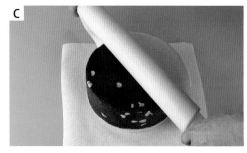

6 Lift up the marzipan over a rolling pin and place over the cake (**C**). Smooth the top of the cake with a smoother, and then gently ease the marzipan down the sides of the cake into position, making sure there are no pleats. Smooth the top curved edge with the palm of your hand and the sides with a smoother.

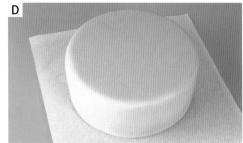

7 Gradually press down with the smoother around the edge of the cake into the excess marzipan, and then trim this away to create a neat edge (**D**). It is best to allow the marzipan to harden in a warm, dry place for 24–48 hours to give a firmer base before decorating, although this is not essential.

Applying a sugarpaste covering

1 For a fruit cake, moisten the surface of the marzipan with clear spirit, such as gin or vodka. Form an even coating; if you leave dry patches, air bubbles may form under the sugarpaste (rolled fondant).

2 For a sponge cake, prepare the cake by covering it with a thin layer of buttercream to fill in any holes and help the sugarpaste stick to the surface of the cake.

3 Knead the sugarpaste until warm and pliable. Roll out on a work surface lightly greased with white vegetable fat (shortening) – this is preferable to using icing sugar because you don't encounter problems with the icing sugar drying out or marking the sugarpaste. Roll the paste to a depth of 5mm (³⁄₁₆in). It is a good idea to use spacers for this, as they ensure an even thickness (**A**).

4 Lift the paste carefully over the top of the cake, supporting it with a rolling pin, and position it so that it covers the cake (**B**). Smooth the surface of the cake to remove any lumps and bumps using a smoother for the flat areas and a combination of smoother and the palm of your hand for the curved ones. Always make sure your hands are clean and dry with no traces of icing sugar before smoothing sugarpaste.

5 Take the smoother and, while pressing down, run the flat edge around the base of the cake to create a cutting line (**C**).

6 Trim away the excess paste with a palette knife (**D**) to create a neat edge.

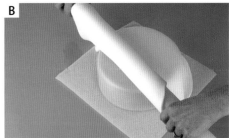

 tip If you find you have unwanted air bubbles under the icing, insert a scriber or clean glass-headed dressmakers' pin at an angle and press out the air.

Covering boards

1 Roll out the sugarpaste to a depth of 4mm (⅛in) or 5mm (³⁄₁₆in), ideally using spacers. Moisten the board with water or sugar glue. Lift up the paste and drape over the board.

2 Circle a smoother over the sugarpaste to achieve a smooth, flat finish to the board. Cut the paste flush with the sides of the board, taking care to keep the edge vertical. The covered board should then be left overnight to dry thoroughly.

Covering the cake board gives your mini cake that professional finishing touch.

Sugar Recipes

Most of the sugar recipes used in the book for covering, modelling and decoration can easily be made at home. Use paste colours to colour them according to the individual project.

Sugarpaste

Ready-made sugarpaste (rolled fondant) is available from supermarkets and cake-decorating suppliers in various colours. It is also easy and inexpensive to make your own.

Ingredients Makes 1kg (2¼lb):
• 60ml (4 tbsp) cold water
• 20ml (4 tsp/1 sachet) powdered gelatine
• 125ml (4fl oz) liquid glucose
• 15ml (1 tbsp) glycerine
• 1kg (2¼lb) icing (confectioners') sugar, sifted, plus extra for dusting

1 Place the water in a small bowl, sprinkle over the gelatine and soak until spongy. Stand the bowl over a pan of hot, but not boiling, water and stir until the gelatine is dissolved. Add the glucose and glycerine, stirring until well blended and runny.

2 Put the icing sugar in a large bowl, make a well in the centre and slowly pour in the liquid ingredients, stirring constantly. Mix well. Turn out onto a surface dusted with icing sugar and knead until smooth, sprinkling with extra icing sugar if the paste becomes too sticky. The paste can be used immediately or tightly wrapped and stored in a plastic bag.

Modelling paste

This versatile paste keeps its shape well, dries harder than sugarpaste (rolled fondant) and is used for adding detail to covered cakes.

Ingredients Makes 225g (8oz):
• 5ml (1 tsp) gum tragacanth
• 225g (8oz) sugarpaste (rolled fondant)

Add the gum tragacanth to the sugarpaste and knead in. Wrap in a plastic bag and allow the gum to work before use. You will begin to feel a difference in the paste after an hour or so, but it is best left overnight. The modelling paste should be firm but pliable with a slight elastic texture. Kneading the modelling paste makes it warm and easy to work with.

Flower paste

Flower paste (petal/gum paste) is available in many varieties. It is possible to make your own, but it is time-consuming and you will need a heavy-duty mixer.

Ingredients Makes 500g (1lb 2oz):
• 500g (1lb 2oz) icing (confectioners') sugar
• 15ml (1 tbsp) gum tragacanth
• 25ml (1½ tbsp) cold water
• 10ml (2 tsp) powered gelatine
• 10ml (2 tsp) liquid glucose
• 15ml (1 tbsp) white vegetable fat (shortening)
• 1 medium egg white

1 Sieve the icing sugar and gum tragacanth into the greased mixing bowl of a heavy-duty mixer.

2 Place the water in a small bowl, sprinkle over the gelatine and soak until spongy. Stand the bowl over a pan of hot but not boiling water and stir until the gelatine has dissolved. Add the glucose and white fat and continue heating until all the ingredients are melted and mixed.

3 Add the glucose mixture and egg white to the icing sugar. Beat very slowly until mixed – at this stage it will be a beige colour – then increase the speed to maximum until the paste becomes white and stringy.

4 Grease your hands and remove the paste from the bowl. Pull and stretch the paste several times, and then knead together. Place in a plastic bag and store in an airtight container. Leave to mature for at least 12 hours.

Colouring paste

To colour paste, place a little paste colour, not liquid colour, onto the end of a cocktail stick (toothpick) or a larger amount onto the end of a palette knife. Add to the paste and knead in thoroughly, adding more until you have the correct result. Be careful with pale colours, as only a little colour is needed.

Pastillage

This is extremely useful because, unlike modelling paste, it sets extremely hard and is not affected by moisture. However, the paste crusts quickly and is brittle once dry. You can buy it in a powdered form, to which you add water, but it is easy to make yourself.

Ingredients Makes 1kg (2¼lb):
• 1 egg white
• 300g (11oz) icing (confectioners') sugar, sifted
• 10ml (2 tsp) gum tragacanth

1 Put the egg white into a large mixing bowl. Gradually add enough icing sugar until the mixture combines together into a ball. Mix in the gum tragacanth, and then turn the paste out onto a work surface and knead the pastillage well.

2 Incorporate the remaining icing sugar into the remainder of pastillage to give a stiff paste.

3 Store pastillage in a polythene bag placed in an airtight container in a refrigerator for up to one month.

Royal icing

Ingredients Makes 1 quantity:
• 1 egg white
• 250g (9oz) icing (confectioners') sugar, sifted.

Put the egg white into a bowl and gradually beat in the icing sugar until the icing is glossy and forms soft peaks.

Sugar glue

Although commercially available, sugar glue is quick and easy to make at home. Break up pieces of white modelling paste into an eggcup or small bowl and cover with boiling water. Stir until dissolved. This produces a thick, strong glue, which can be easily thinned by adding some more cooled boiled water.

Confectioners' glaze

Used where a glossy-looking sheen is needed and where a surface needs sealing. Confectioners' glaze is available from cake-decorating suppliers.

Buttercream

Use buttercream to sandwich cakes together, to coat them before covering with sugarpaste (rolled fondant) or on its own as a cake covering.

Ingredients Makes 1 quantity:
• 110g (3¾oz) unsalted (sweet) butter
• 350g (12oz) icing (confectioners') sugar
• 15–30ml (1–2 tbsp) milk or water
• a few drops of vanilla extract or alternative flavouring

1 Place the butter in a bowl and beat until the texture is light and fluffy.

2 Sift the icing sugar into the bowl and continue to beat until the mixture changes colour. Add just enough milk or water to give a firm but spreadable consistency.

3 Flavour by adding the vanilla or alternative flavouring, then store in an airtight container until required.

Chocolate buttercream

To make chocolate buttercream, follow the buttercream recipe above and mix 30ml (2 tbsp) of unsweetened cocoa powder with the milk or water before adding it to the butter and sugar mixture. Omit the flavourings.

White chocolate buttercream

Ingredients Makes 1 quantity:
• 115g (4oz) white chocolate
• 115g (4oz) unsalted (sweet) butter
• 225g (8oz) icing (confectioners') sugar

Melt the chocolate in a bowl over a pan of hot water and leave to cool slightly. Soften the butter and beat in the sugar, and then beat in the chocolate.

tip *For those on a dairy-free diet, make white buttercream by replacing the butter with solid white vegetable fat (shortening).*

White vegetable fat (shortening)

This is a solid white vegetable fat, which is often known by a brand name: in the UK, Trex or White Flora; in South Africa, Holsum; in Australia, Copha; and in America, Crisco. These products are more or less interchangeable in cake making.

Cake jewellery: the basics

Some of the most dramatic cakes in the book are decorated with toppers, crowns or garlands made of different weights and colours of wires and a variety of beads. The effects you can achieve are endless once you have some basic knowledge about the tools and equipment you will need.

Basic tools

You don't need many tools to be able to create effective cake jewellery:

- Wire cutters (essential)
- Jewellery pliers (essential)
- Round-nose pliers (used to make coils)
- Bead mat (to prevent beads from rolling)

Glue

You will need a strong acrylic-based non-toxic glue, available from most bead and jewellery-making suppliers.

Wires

It is important that you use the right wire for your jewellery. The wires used in cake jewellery can easily be split into groups:

Soft beading/binding wires

These are soft wires that are used in the creation of cake crowns and beaded garlands. They include the following:

- **Beading wire**, 28 gauge is a cheap, widely-available wire (**1**).

- **Coloured craft wire**, 0.3mm, is a smooth enamelled wire, available in many colours, ideal for creating cake crown elements.

- **Bullion wire**, a crinkly wire, used in many crafts; here it is usually used to make beaded garlands (**2**).

Note: Silver tends to tarnish (oxidise) once exposed to the air, so store your silver cake jewellery carefully. To prevent tarnishing over a long period of time, firstly wrap the jewellery in tissue paper, then place in an airtight bag and store in a dark, dry place.

Intermediate wires

These are stronger wires that can support a little weight; they are used for wired cake toppers and elements of cake crowns.

- **Coloured craft wire**, 0.5mm (25g SWG/24g AWG), is a smooth enamelled wire, available in many colours, ideal for coils and bead support on cake crowns. It is also thin enough to go through the holes in most beads so it lends itself to beaded cake topper creations (**3**).

- **Metallic reel**, 0.5mm (0.020in), is similar to the above but manufactured for the floristry industry and has a steel core rather than copper making this wire stiffer; ideal when heavy beads are being used (**4**).

- **Straight, paper-covered, floristry wire**, available in many gauges with 24 gauge being the recommend strength for cake fountains. This wire is not suitable for cake crowns (**5**).

Strong wires

This heavy-duty wire is used for the base of cake crowns:

- **1.2mm (18g SWG/17g AWG) jewellery wire**, the wire that you bind all your cake crown elements to (**6**).

Aluminium wire

This is available in many widths, but for cake decorations the best ones to use are 1.5mm (16g or 17g SWG/52g AWG) and 2mm (14g SWG/12g AWG). The wire can be easily bent to create any shape you wish; it is also available in an ever increasing range of colours, opening up many possibilities for cake decorators (**7**).

Beads

There is a huge choice of beads available from around the world, ranging from cheap plastic to expensive crystal. Which beads you choose for your cake project will depend on your budget and the effect you are trying to create.

Delicate and colourful, wired-bead trims and crowns on cakes are becoming extremely popular with brides, who often base the design for their cake crown on their wedding tiara. But the decorations can also be the perfect finish for celebration cakes for all kinds of occasions.

Your choice of colours and beads will create the mood: soft pastels and pearls make ideal decorations for a traditional style of wedding, whereas fiery reds and oranges would suit a birthday cake. How you bend the wires will also change the appearance of the decoration.

mm	SWG	AWG	Inches
0.2mm	36g	32g	0.0076
0.3mm	31g	29g	0.0116
0.4mm	27g	26g	0.0164
0.5mm	25g	24g	0.0200
0.6mm	23g	22g	0.0240
0.8mm	21g	20g	0.0320
1mm	19g	18g	0.0400
1.2mm	18g	17g	0.0480
1.5mm	16g/17g	15g	0.0600
2mm	14g	12g	0.0800

SWG: standard wire gauge (as used in the UK)
AWG: American wire gauge

Sizes

Beads range in size from the tiny seed beads to large beads designed to be worn as pendants. Those measuring 6mm (¼in) and 8mm (⁵⁄₁₆in) tend to be the most frequently used in cake jewellery, although smaller beads such as silver-lined Japanese rocailles are used to add sparkle, and larger beads such as 12mm (¹⁵⁄₃₂in) pearls are added to create focal points.

Shapes

Most people think of beads as round, but of course they are available in a variety of shapes. Round beads are the most frequently used for cake jewellery, but heart, star and cut crystal shapes are often appropriate, too.

A mix of colours

Cake jewellery is most effective when it reflects the other colours used on the cake, including the icing. So, for example, if a cake is covered with an ivory icing, it helps to have a few ivory pearls in the jewellery to bring the design together. Blending and contrasting colour schemes also work well.

Selecting beads

It is a good idea to place the beads you have chosen for a project on a bead mat or small tray so that you can see what they look like together. This also enables you to add or remove beads or colours to achieve a balance between the colours and shapes that you are happy with.

Celebration

Hearts & Flowers

Valentine's Day is the most romantic day of the year and there is no better way to celebrate it than to say it with flowers. And for sweethearts with a sweet tooth, combining flowers with cake is guaranteed to be a hit! These perfectly pink mini cakes are so quick and easy to make, you can soon create a large batch to share with the one you love.

If you are feeling a little more creative, you can extend the floral theme by using the sugarpaste flowers to make a beautiful topper, perfect for adorning your cake designs. See page 27 for how to create a bright and bold cake topped with an array of beautiful flowers, ideal for celebrating Mother's Day or a springtime birthday.

The flowers are simply created using blossom cutters and can be attached in a pattern of your choice using sugar glue for simply stunning results.

you will need ...

materials

- sugarpaste (rolled fondant): dark pink
- white vegetable fat (shortening)
- cakes: Heart Mini cake and Petite Heart pans (W)
- buttercream (see page 19)
- modelling paste: pink
- sugar glue (see page 19)

equipment

- blossom cutters: 5cm (2in) (FMM Large Blossom set), 2.5cm (1in) (FMM Large Blossom set), 1.3cm (½in) (PME plunger set)

Preparing the cakes

1 Bake your cakes in Heart Mini cake and Petite Heart pans (see pages 12–14).

2 Cover the cakes with buttercream and then dark pink sugarpaste (see page 17). Leave to dry.

Making the flowers

1 Roll out the pale pink modelling paste and cut large flowers and medium flowers using blossom cutters (**A**) and a selection of smaller flowers using blossom plunger cutters.

2 Add the flower centres by rolling darker pink sugarpaste balls of an appropriate size and placing them in the centre of each flower. Attach these onto the flowers using sugar glue. Attach the flowers onto the cake in various positions using sugar glue.

A

Floral Fun

Take the floral theme one step further by adding a bold floral topper to instantly brighten up your cake. It is quick to make and looks fantastic on a single tier, decorated with stylish modelling paste flowers in coordinating colours.

Roll out the pink and ivory modelling paste between narrow spacers. Then, using the five petal blossom cutter, cut out three of each colour. Press the pointed end of a Dresden tool between each petal and drag the paste towards the middle to create more rounded petals (B). Place the flower on a foam pad or in the palm of your hand. Press into the centre of each petal with the small end of a ball tool to create a cupped effect (C).

Make the centres by pressing a small ball of yellow modelling paste into a daisy centre mould (D). Attach the centres then dip one end of some short lengths of 20-gauge wire into sugar glue and insert a wire into the side of each flower between two petals. Leave to dry horizontally, ideally on foam.

To arrange the topper, place a small amount of oasis fix into the posy pick to help secure the wires. Take a wired flower and curve the wire to shape. Cut to an appropriate length and insert into the posy pick. Create the basic shape of the topper then infill with the remaining flowers.

Fine Wine

These elegant mini cakes make inspiring gifts for wine lovers, or anyone who enjoys a glass or two. Painted realistically, the bottles appear to contain wine and are complete with detailed labels to add an authentic touch. The lid and bottle tops are gilded with bronze edible lustre dust, providing a luxurious highlight to these little works of art.

Create these smart presentation boxes of fine wines as a birthday, celebration or retirement gift for a connoisseur or wine enthusiast. There is a lot of scope for personalizing the cakes by adding names and dates, or even modelling the bottles on the recipient's favourite tipple.

Although the bottle details might seem complicated, the shape is simply created using a cutter and you can resize and trace the labels from magazine pictures or the Internet.

you will need . . .

materials

- sugarpaste (rolled fondant): bottle green, ivory, gold
- cakes to cut into 9 x 3.5 x 3cm (3½in x 1⅜in x 1⅛in) portions
- sugar glue (see page 19)
- modelling paste: bottle green, ivory, cream, olive green

- paste colours: mint green, olive green, golden brown (Spectral autumn leaf), cream, red, black
- edible dust colours: bronze, selection of golds
- confectioners' glaze

equipment

- smoother
- palette knife
- scriber
- straight edge, such as a ruler
- set square
- narrow spacers
- 1.5mm (¹⁄₁₆in) spacers – made from thick card
- craft knife

- cutting wheel
- Dresden tool
- paintbrushes
- Small bottle cutter (PC)
- small embosser, such as Embossing Sticks – set 2 (HP) (optional)
- Edible pens (optional)

Preparing the cakes

1 Cut your cake (see pages 12–14) into 9 x 3.5 x 3cm (3½ x 1⅜ x 1⅛in) portions. Place a cake on waxed paper so that it rests on one of the largest sides – the back or front of the cake.

2 Knead the bottle-green sugarpaste until warm. Roll just over half into a roughly rectangular shape between 1.5mm (¹⁄₁₆in) spacers. Cut one long edge straight.

tip

To stick the sugarpaste to the cake, cover one side at a time with a thin layer of buttercream.

3 Lift the green sugarpaste and position over the side of the cake, placing the straight edge against the lower edge. Use a smoother to ensure the sugarpaste is flat and vertical, then roughly cut away the excess paste with a pair of scissors to remove the excess weight (**A**).

4 Place the smoother onto the surface of the green sugarpaste then, using a palette knife, remove the excess paste by cutting away from the cake onto the smoother (**B**). Repeat for the second green side.

5 Cover the uppermost side with ivory sugarpaste. Move the cake back into its upright position and cover the remaining side and top with ivory sugarpaste. Allow to dry.

Decorating the cakes
Adding the lid

1 Scribe a horizontal line onto each green side of the cake to mark the lid of the box, using a set square (**C**).

2 Knead the gold sugarpaste, then roll out some into a rectangular shape between 1.5mm (¹⁄₁₆in) spacers. Cut one long edge straight (**D**). Paint over the narrow green sides of the lid with sugar glue, then place the cut edge along one of the scribed lines. Cut away the majority of the excess paste with scissors then cut to shape by using a smoother and palette knife. Cover the other narrow end, followed by the two sides ensuring that the corners of the lid remain sharp.

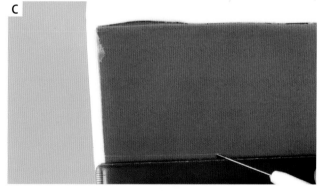

3 To emboss the lid, mark near the outside edges of each face at 2mm (³/₁₆in) vertical intervals using a ruler and scriber. Line up the marks horizontally with a straight edge, and emboss the sugarpaste repeatedly to create the textured pattern of the lid (**E**). Repeat for the remaining sides.

4 Cover the top of the cake, neatening the cut edges so that they become part of the pattern of the lid.

5 Mix up a quantity of dark/antique gold and, using a flat-headed brush, paint the lid of the box using long horizontal strokes (**F**).

Creating the bottles

1 Roll out modelling paste in a selection of suitable bottle, foil and label colours using narrow spacers.

2 Emboss the bottles design onto the rolled out pastes using the bottle cutter. Using a craft knife held vertically, cut along the embossed lines of the shapes.

3 Attach modelling paste pieces in suitable colours onto the cake using sugar glue. Ensure that the sections abut neatly.

E

F

tip

Personalize your design by using the recipient's favourite wines or drink. Find pictures of the bottles and scale down to use as templates.

Painting labels

1 In a paint palette separately dilute some mint green and olive green paste colours with clear spirit. Then with a soft paintbrush carefully apply a colour wash to the glass sections of the bottle.

2 Slightly dilute a section of suitable paste colours in clear spirit. Then using a fine paintbrush, add painted detail to the labels (**G**). Alternatively, use edible pens to add your details. Use these examples of real bottle labels for reference. You can also personalize your designs by adding suitable names, dates, places and so on.

3 Mix a little bronze edible lustre dust with some confectioners' glaze and use to paint over one of the bottle tops. Individually mix up the various golds and colour the remaining bottle tops.

4 Take a fine paintbrush and add gold detail to the labels and foils as required.

tip

Clean your brush immediately after painting with glaze.

Floral Fountain

Decorating a simple cake with a beadwork designs instantly adds a touch of elegance. By delicately threading beautiful beads and flowers onto fine wires you can create sparkling ornamental jewellery to brighten up the simplest of designs. The eye-catching topper, with its beautiful beads, flowers and pearls also adds a striking sense of height and movement.

Wired-bead trims and crowns on cakes are becoming extremely popular with brides, who often use their wedding tiara for inspiration. Your choice of colours and beads will create the mood for the cake. Here the striking red and gold beads combine beautifully with the delicate wire flowers and pearls for an opulent and luxurious feel.

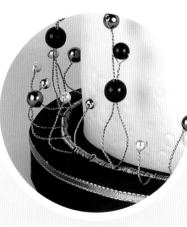

Aim for a stress-free celebration by making the ornaments in advance, leaving the simple icing and final stages until nearer the big day.

you will need ...

materials

- sugarpaste (rolled fondant): ivory and red
- cakes: 10cm (4in) round
- buttercream (see page 19) or apricot glaze and marzipan (see page 16)
- beads: 8mm (⁵/₁₆in) red wooden; 6mm (¼in) pearls, ivory, bronze and red; 4mm (¹/₈in) pearls, ivory and gold
- gold wire flowers with ruby glass centres
- wires: 1.2mm (18g SWG/17g AWG) strong gold-plated wire; 0.3mm (31g SWG/29g AWG) gold coloured craft wire, 24 gauge floristry wire

equipment

- 17.5cm (7in) cake drum/board
- smoother
- palette knife
- wire cutters
- round-nosed pliers
- flat-nosed pliers
- posy pick
- oasis fix
- Flower cutters e.g. Flat floral collection (LC)
- piping tubes e.g. PME no. 4, 16, 17, 18
- acrylic glue
- cocktail stick or toothpick
- jewel glue (optional)

Preparing the cakes

1 Cover the cake drum with red sugarpaste (see page 17).

2 Cover the cake (see pages 12–14) with ivory sugarpaste (see page 17) and emboss the sugarpaste, whilst still soft, with a suitable flower cutter and a selection of round piping tubes. Once dry, place the cake in the centre of the covered board.

Creating the crowns

1 Cut 15cm (6in) lengths of the 0.3mm gold coloured craft wire. Take a bead and thread it onto of the cut lengths. Using your thumb and index finger of one hand, hold the bead in the middle of the wire then bring the wires together between your thumb and index finger of your other hand so the bead is locked in place. Twist the bead repeatedly whilst slowly allowing the wire in your other hand to slide through your fingers for an even twist. Twist to the desired length and separate the wires to form a 'T' shape (**A**). Repeat.

2 Thread two stems through the hole of another bead, then reposition the wires to create the required 'T' shape.

tip

The secret of an even twist is releasing the wire with even pressure.

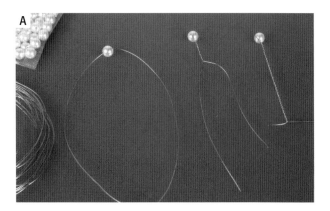

A

3 Cut a length of strong jewellery wire to form the band at least 1–2cm (⅜–¾in) larger than the diameter of the covered cake. Starting near one end, hold one of the prepared wire 'T' shapes onto the strong wire and wrap the 0.3mm craft wire around both wires on one side of the 'T' to bind the two neatly together. Hold the next 'T' in place then neatly wrap the beading wire around all wires so they are all bound securely in place. Continue this process, adding the 'T' shapes at regular intervals.

4 To join the crown together, continue binding until you reach the end of the wire then abut the two ends of the strong wire and continue binding the 'T's until you reach your start point.

5 If necessary, adjust the shape of the base of the crown to create a circle. Slide the anchor beads of the double stems up and open out the stems so the anchor beads sits 2cm (¾in) above the base of the crown. Place the completed crown carefully over the cake to rest on the cake board.

Making the beaded toppers

1 To attach the beads and wire flowers, dip the end of a 24-gauge floristry wire into acrylic glue and place a bead on top of the glue. Leave horizontally to dry. To create wires with several beads, use a cocktail stick (toothpick) to place a dot of glue on the wire for the bead furthest from the end. Thread the bead onto the wire so that it rests on the glue dot. Make different combinations of beaded wires as before (**B**).

2 Insert the posy pick vertically into the centre of the cake so that its top lies flush with the top of the sugarpaste covering the cake (**C**).

3 Place a little oasis fix into the posy pick. Take a beaded wire and gently curve the wire by wrapping it around a cylinder such as a can or roll of tape (**D**). Cut the wire as appropriate and insert it into the posy pick. Repeat with the other wire lengths, creating the shape of the topper with a few straight-wired beads that define the height and adding curved wires around the base of the fountain.

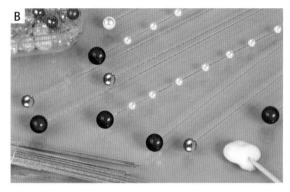

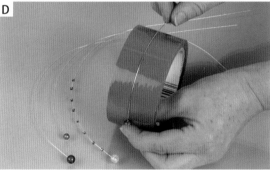

tip

It helps to stand back occasionally while arranging the wires to get an overall impression of the shape.

Pretty In Pink

One of the most exquisite flowers, the moth orchid, is the focal point of these stunning mini cakes. The delicate orchid petals are easily created using special cutters and flower paste, yet they are stunning in their realistic appearance. The soft pastel pink shades are so feminine and really enhance the beauty of the blooms.

These stylish mini cakes make ideal individual gifts for the guests at a bridal party – you can even match the colour scheme to the fabric of the bride's or bridesmaids' outfit. Alternatively, you can use moth orchids to add a feminine touch to a birthday cake or Mother's Day gift.

The beautiful flowers are so life-like in appearance, perfectly created using special moth orchid cutters and finely painted details.

you will need ...

materials

- sugarpaste (rolled fondant): pale pink, pink, white with a touch of pink
- royal icing
- white vegetable fat (shortening)
- cakes: 3cm (1⅛in) deep slices
- buttercream (see page 19) or apricot glaze and marzipan (see pages 16)

- paste colours: claret (SF)
- flower paste (petal/gum paste): white or dark pink
- edible dust colours: plum, deep yellow, snowflake (SK)

equipment

- 6.5cm (2½in) wide six-petal blossom cutter
- smoother
- palette knife
- selection of brushes including a fine tip and a dusting brush
- sugar shaper with medium round disc

- life-size moth orchid cutter set (LC)
- clear plastic, such as a plastic bag
- ball tool
- moth orchid veiner (GM05N505-01)
- dimpled foam
- foam pad

Preparing the cakes

1 Cut a cake into 3cm (1⅛in) deep slices (see pages 12–14). Use a 6.5cm (2½in) wide six-petal blossom cutter to cut out as many mini cakes as required. Cover each cake with pink sugarpaste (see page 17). Leave to dry.

2 Add pink trim to the base of each minicake using the sugar shaper and small round disc. To do this, soften the pink modelling paste by kneading in some white vegetable fat to stop the paste getting sticky. Partially dunk the paste into a small container of boiled water before kneading again until paste becomes really soft and stretchy.

tip

Another way to soften the modelling paste is to put the barrel of the shaper full of paste into a microwave for about six seconds. Use immediately before the paste cools.

Creating the moth orchids

1 Smear white vegetable fat over your work board to prevent
sticking. Roll out some white or dark pink flower paste very
thinly – you should be able to see your workboard through the
paste. Using the moth orchid cutters, cut one dorsal (central)
sepal, two lateral (lower) sepals and two petals (the largest
cutter). Tint some flower paste pink and cut out one lip for each
flower. Cover with clear plastic to prevent them from drying out.

2 Place a sepal onto the foam pad. Using the ball tool, stroke
around the edges of the paste by pressing the tool half on
the paste and half on the pad to soften the cut edge. Place the
sepal in the double-sided moth orchid veiner. Press down hard
on the top of the veiner then release (**A**). Remove the paste.
Place the sepal onto dimpled foam and leave to dry partially.
Repeat for the remaining sepals and petals.

3 Arrange the sepals and petals in groups as shown (**B**).
Attach them onto the mini cakes using royal icing so that
the top and lateral sepals lie under the larger side petals.

4 For the lip, soften the edges of the paste with a ball tool
then cup the two side lobes by gently circling a ball tool in
their centres. Roll three tiny sausages of paste, add two for the
callus and one onto the tip of the lip for the lip tendril (**C**). Using
a dry dusting brush, dip the tip of the brush into a pot of plum
dust, tap off the excess and dust the edges of the lip. Add deep
yellow dust to the centre.

5 Dilute some claret paste colour in clear spirit and add
markings using a fine paintbrush. Place the lips onto the
cupped area of dimpled foam and allow to dry sufficiently so
that the cupped shape is maintained when handled.

6 Place a dot of royal icing in the centre of each flower on the
cake and attach the lips in place. Roll small balls of white
flower paste and stick onto the central point of each flower to
represent a pearl. Dilute some snowflake dust in clear spirit and
paint over each pearl.

A

B
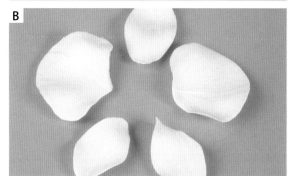

C

tip

*Try to arrange the flowers while
there is still some flexibility in the
flower paste; once they are dry
they are very brittle.*

Shimmering Snowflakes

One of the many amazing wonders of the natural world is the tiny snowflake – an individual crystalline work of art. No two snowflakes are ever alike and each is inspiring in their beauty and delicacy. Snowflakes make a wonderful addition to a simple mini cake design, and as each one is individual you can be as creative as you like with your designs.

These glistening snowy-white mini cakes are beautifully decorated with individual delicate snowflakes, each one displaying its own unique pattern. They make a fantastic alternative to the traditional Christmas cake or could be given as favours at a winter wedding to really impress your guests.

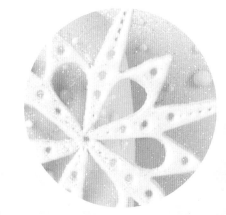

Made from pastillage, these delicate snowflakes are easily created using cutters. They can be decorated using small cutters and quilting tools to create a variety of interesting and individual patterns.

you will need ...

materials

- superwhite dust (SF) (optional)
- sugarpaste (rolled fondant): white
- royal icing
- icing (confectioners') sugar (optional)
- white vegetable fat (shortening)
- cakes: 5cm (2in) mulitmini cake pans

- pastillage: white
- buttercream (see page 19) or apricot glaze and marzipan (see page 16)
- clear spirit, such as gin or vodka
- dust colours: sparkles (SK) and/ or snowflake (SK)

equipment

- smoother
- palette knife
- narrow spacers made from 1.5mm (1/16in) thick card
- snowflake cutters, such as: starburst snowflake (LC), intricate snowflake (LC), simple snowflake (LC)
- selection of small cutters to remove patterns from the snowflakes, such as: small teardrop

(LC), small triangle (LC), micro leaf cutter, small blossom
- craft knife
- quilting tool
- piping tubes (tips) no. 16, 4, 2, 1
- paintbrushes
- cocktail stick (toothpick)
- reusable piping bag and coupler
- glass-headed dressmakers' pins

Preparing the cakes

1 Bake your cakes in 5cm (2in) multimini cake pans or cut a larger cake into 5cm (2in) deep slices (see pages 12–14). Using a 5cm (2in) circle cutter, cut the slices into rounds.

2 Cover the cakes with the white sugarpaste (see page 17). Leave to dry.

tip

Knead some superwhite dust (edible whitening powder) into your sugarpaste to make it look as pure white as snow.

Creating the snowflakes

There are many different types of snowflakes with each one being unique, so below are some ideas for creating individual crystalline shapes. Firstly whiten the pastillage by kneading in some superwhite dust, then use to create your crystals.

1 To create the outline shape of your snowflake, begin by rolling out some of the pastillage between the narrow spacers. Pick up the paste and place it over the intricate snowflake cutter, then roll over the paste with a rolling pin (**A**). Run your finger over the edges of the cutter, then turn the cutter over and carefully press out the pastillage onto a well-greased work board.

2 Take a quilting tool and run it across the resulting snowflake from point to opposite point (**B**). Add texture to its surface using a soft paintbrush.

3 Cut a circle from the centre of each of the six inner sections, as defined by the quilting tool, using the end of a no. 16 piping tube (**C**).

4 Leave the snowflakes on your work board until the paste has hardened, to prevent them distorting. Place on a foam pad and dry thoroughly.

Other Ideas

Cut out a snowflake shape as before using the starburst cutter. Some snowflakes have what look like feathered edges; to create this on your snowflakes take a sharp craft knife and make repeated small cuts into the edges (**D**).

Adding the snowflakes

Carefully attach the dried pastillage snowflakes to the cake using royal icing. Support the snowflakes on the sides of the cake with pins to prevent them slipping down before the royal icing has set. Remove the pins once secure (**E**).

E

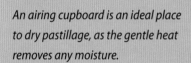

tip

An airing cupboard is an ideal place to dry pastillage, as the gentle heat removes any moisture.

F

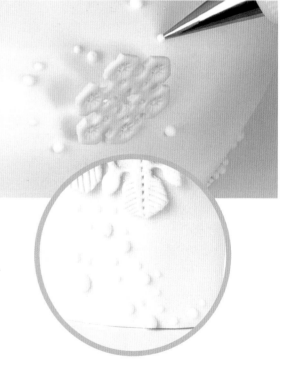

Adding snow

1 Fit the no. 16 tube into the coupler on the reusable piping bag and half fill the bag with whitened royal icing. Pipe a few dots then change the tube and pipe more dots. Continue changing the tube and piping dots in different sizes to create a random pattern of dots around the snowflakes to look like drifting snow (**F**). Allow the icing to set.

2 Dust the cake and snowflakes with either or both of the suggested dusts to add a real sparkle to the appearance of the cake.

tip

Check the consistency of your icing and adjust as necessary – you need to be able to pipe dots, not pointed cones.

Icy ideas

Get creative and make every snowflake individual by using different cutters to vary the outline shapes, such as the starburst and simple snowflake cutters used here. Try combining or overlapping cutters to create different shapes and removing paste away from the outline of the shape using a part of a cutter to create a variety of interesting patterns. For example, you can use a small teardrop cutter and cut out six shapes radiating out from the centre for stunning results, or try creating a more delicate floral pattern using the end of a no. 16 piping tube for a beautiful lacy effect.

Fun & Funky

Shocking pink, luminous orange and bright yellow shout out from these vibrant mini cakes made from stacked square cakes cut at angles to give an entirely individual effect. They are original designs, perfect for those who like something different. Bold statements and wild colours create simple but eye-catching decorations, which are all simply made using cutters.

If you know someone who's a little on the wild side, make them the perfect gift with this funky design. By adding tall coordinated candles, they make fabulous birthday gifts for an outgoing girl on her eighteenth birthday, or they could even be favours for a fun-loving and extravert couple's wedding.

The concentric circles are surprisingly easy to create and can be instantly transformed into bold floral designs by simply adding small circles of modelling paste around them.

you will need ...

materials

- sugarpaste (rolled fondant): orange, red, pink
- white vegetable fat (shortening)
- cakes: cut into 9cm (3½in), 6cm (2⅜in) and 3cm (1⅛in) squares
- buttercream (see page 19)
- royal icing
- modelling paste: red, orange, pink, yellow, purple
- sugar glue (see page 19)

equipment

- 5mm (³⁄₁₆in) spacers
- 15cm (6in) round cake drum/board
- smoother
- palette knife
- waxed paper
- sugar shaper and medium round disc
- fine paintbrush
- craft knife
- Dresden tool
- narrow spacers made from 1.5mm (¹⁄₁₆in) thick card
- circle cutters
- clear plastic, such as a plastic bag
- piping tubes (tips) nos 18, 16, 4 (PME)
- orange ribbon and non-toxic glue stick

Preparing the cakes

1 Use square templates to carve your mini cakes (see pages 12–14) into 9cm (3½in), 6cm (2⅜in) and 3cm (1⅛in) squares. Make the heights of the cakes 6.5cm (2½in), 5cm (2in) and 3.5cm (1⅜in) respectively.

2 Take a sharp knife and a ruler, and vertically make a cut diagonally through one cake from the top corner on one side to 4cm (1½in), 3cm (⅛in) and 2.5cm (1in) respectively below the top corner on the other (**A**). Then turn the cakes over and cut their sides so they all slope (**B**).

3 Cover the board using orange sugarpaste (see page 17). Place the carved cakes on waxed paper and cover with buttercream. Use red sugarpaste to cover the 9cm (3½in) cake, orange for the 6cm (2⅜in) cake and pink for the 3cm (1⅛in) cake (see page 17).

4 Place the base tier centrally on the prepared cake drum. Using a small amount of royal icing, stack the tiers using the main picture for guidance.

5 With a fine paintbrush paint a line of sugar glue around the base of each cake. Use a sugar shaper to squeeze lengths of softened modelling paste over these lines. Glue the ends together and blend the join with the wide end of a Dresden tool.

A

B

tip

When joining the trim, cut both ends of the sugarpaste at 45 degrees using a craft knife so that the two ends will fit snugly.

Fun & Funky *51*

Decorating the cakes

1 Roll out the different colours of modelling paste between narrow spacers and cover with plastic to prevent them from drying out. Using a circle cutter, cut a circle from one of the pastes. Use a smaller circle cutter to remove a circle from the centre of the larger one. Replace this circle with one of a different colour, and blend the join between the two circles by rubbing a finger over the pastes so that there is no gap between them (**C**).

2 Continue removing and replacing circles of different colours using the piping tubes as circle cutters. Attach the concentric circles to the cake using sugar glue.

3 Using the piping tubes, cut small circles of paste in different colours and sizes (**D**) and attach them around the outside of some of the circles on the cake using sugar glue. Insert a tall candle to the concentric circle positioned on the top of the cake.

4 Using a non-toxic glue stick, attach the ribbon around the sides of the board to complete the cake.

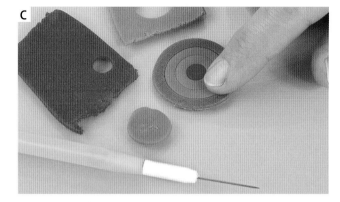

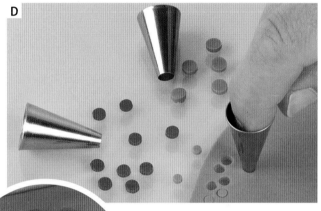

tip

A scriber is an excellent tool to help remove the cut circles. Where the circles on the sides abut the base of the cake, cut across a section of the circle with a craft knife for a close fit.

Designer

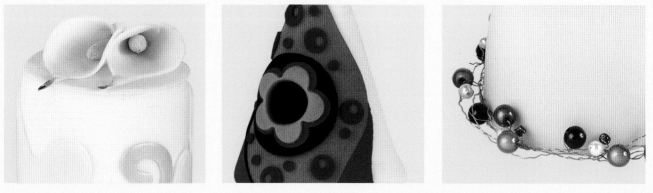

Op Art Minis

These eye-catching miniature creations capture the 1960s when bold black-and-white designs, called Op Art, took the fashion and interior design worlds by storm. Smart and sophisticated, these mini cakes are decorated in a stunning retro style, with some faces plain and others decorated with the contrasting themes of flat floral patterns and bold stripes.

These mini cakes would make an ideal gift for anyone with an eye for style or for someone who loves the 1960s. You don't have to stop at flowers and stripes; try introducing other geometric patterns in black or white, or why not introduce some colour for an even bolder display?

The decoration is surprisingly straightforward to make – just be careful to keep the stripes straight.

you will need ...

materials

- sugarpaste (rolled fondant): white, black
- cakes: 5cm (2in) squares x 3.5cm (1³⁄₈in) deep
- buttercream (see page 19), or apricot glaze and marzipan (see page 16)
- clear spirit, such as gin or vodka (if using fruit cake)
- modelling paste: black, white
- sugar glue (see page 19)

equipment

- smoother
- palette knife
- narrow spacers made from 1.5mm (¹⁄₁₆in) thick card
- craft knife
- piping tubes (tips), no 18, 16, 4, 2 (PME)
- flower cutters: five-petal and eight-petal flat floral cutters (PME), small plunger blossom cutters (PME), flat floral collection set 1 (LC)

Preparing the cakes

1 Bake your cakes and cut them into 5cm (2in) squares x 3.5cm (1³⁄₈in) deep (see pages 12–14).

2 Cover one side of the mini cakes with sugarpaste at a time. Roll out some sugarpaste between 1.5mm (¹⁄₁₆in) spacers and cut the paste in half lengthways. Cover one side of the cake with a thin layer of buttercream. Lift up one half of the sugarpaste and position over the side of the cake, placing the straight edge against the lower edge of the cake. Take a smoother and smooth the paste to give an even surface. Roughly cut away the excess paste with a pair of scissors.

tip

At this stage you are just removing the excess weight from the sugarpaste, not trying to achieve a neat finish.

3 Place the smoother onto the surface of the sugarpaste. Using a palette knife, remove the excess paste by cutting away from the cake onto the smoother (**A**).

4 For the second side, make a cut at right angles to the straight edge of the remaining sugarpaste then position the sugarpaste on the cake so that the edges abut. Trim as for the first side then straighten the corner with a smoother (**B**).

5 Repeat for the remaining sides and top of the cake. For the top of the cake you will have to cut upwards against the smoother (**C**).

tip

Wash your hands and wipe your board when changing colour to prevent your paste turning grey.

Creating the floral design

Making the large accent flowers

1 Roll out some white modelling paste and cut out a flower using the five-petal flat floral cutter and another using the eight-petal flat floral cutter. Place a smoother over the flowers and press down on the paste to enlarge them fractionally.

2 Cut out the same flower shape from thinly rolled black modelling paste and allow the paste to harden for a few minutes. Paint sugar glue over the white flowers then, using a palette knife, lift the black flowers and place them carefully over the white flowers so that a rim of white shows around the black (**D**).

3 Attach the flowers to the cake using sugar glue, referring to the picture for placement. Create some flower centres, using circles cut from white modelling paste and attach using sugar glue.

tip

Where the flowers overlap the edges of the cake, cut away the excess paste using a craft knife.

Making the smaller flowers

1 Thinly roll out some white modelling paste and cut out small, six-petal blossoms using the smallest cutter from the flat floral collection and five-petal blossoms using the small blossom plunger set or similar.

2 Using a no. 4 tube, cut black circles. Add these to the centres of the six-petal blossoms. For the white blossom remove the centre of each flower with a no. 2 tube. Cut a few black blossoms using the smallest plunger cutter and add a white centre to each. Attach the blossoms to the cake, referring to the picture for guidance.

Creating the striped design

1 Thinly roll out some black and white modelling paste between narrow spacers. Cut one edge of each colour straight then, using a set square and a craft knife, cut strips of varying thicknesses from each colour (**E**).

2 Paint over one side of the cake with sugar glue and place the first vertical strip in position at one corner, draping the excess paste over the top of the cake. Add a second strip in the contrasting colour and continue until the side is covered. Next, take a craft knife and, holding it horizontally, carefully remove the excess paste from the top of the cake (**F**).

3 Create dots in one or two of the stripes by removing circles using small piping tubes (**G**). Replace the circles in the white stripes with black ones cut from thinly rolled paste using the same size tube. Continue until all the sides of the cake are covered.

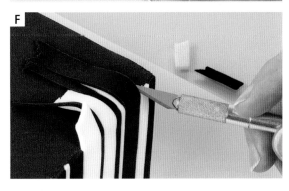

tip

You could vary the design by cutting larger circle, triangular or diamond shapes within the stripes using cutters or a craft knife and inserting sugarpaste of a contrasting colour.

Note Perfect

These mini musical delights are tinted in elegant sepia shades and can be topped in a variety of ways for striking effects. Musical notes and trebles clefs make fantastic toppers for music lovers and their antique gold dust gilding makes an immediate impact against the cream base shades. Piped champagne bubbles create a real sense of occasion, and the delicate beaded copper-wired crowns and toppers add a lavish finishing touch.

These simple mini cakes can be instantly transformed into an extravaganza to celebrate the success of a student or professional musician. With their luxurious cream and gold colouring, they also would make perfect wedding favours for a couple that love music, or to celebrate a golden wedding.

The musical notes are so quick to create using a special cutter, yet they make a harmonious addition to any cake design.

you will need ...

materials

- white sugarpaste (rolled fondant)
- paste colours: golden brown (Spectral – autumn leaf), chestnut brown (Spectral – chestnut)
- cakes: 5cm (2in) deep slices, 5cm (2in) mulitmini cake pans (optional) (see pages 12–14)

- buttercream (see page 19)
- royal icing
- antique gold (SK) edible dust colour
- confectioners' glaze

equipment

- smoother
- palette knife
- piping bags
- piping tubes no.s 2, 3 and 4
- musical notes and treble clef cutters (FMM)
- paintbrushes

For the garland and crown

- an assortment of beads; Lindy used:
- 4mm (⅛in) and 6mm (¼in) ivory pearls, 6mm (¼in) rich-brown wooden beads, chocolate silver-lined rocailles, 6mm (¼in) burnt-orange miracle beads, 6mm (¼in) and 8mm (⁵⁄₁₆in) amber miracle beads
- copper bullion wire
- 0.3mm and 0.5mm antique gold coloured craft wire
- strong 1mm (19g SWG/18g AWG) width copper jewellery wire
- wire cutters
- round-nosed pliers

Preparing the cakes

1 Bake your cakes using 5cm (2in) multimini cake pans, or if necessary, cut a cake into 5cm (2in) deep slices (see pages 12–14). Using a 5cm (2in) circle cutter, cut the slices into rounds.

2 Create different tones of sepia-coloured sugarpaste by adding a little golden brown and chestnut brown to white sugarpaste. Cover the cakes with buttercream and then sugarpaste (see page 17) and leave to dry.

Decorating the cakes

Use the following techniques as inspiration for decorating your own cakes as you wish, using a variety of cutters and pastes to achieve different effects.

Creating the musical notes and clefs

Colour the pastillage gold using the golden brown paste colour. Using the musical cutters (FMM), cut out musical notes and a treble clef. Place on foam to dry. Mix some edible gold dust with confectioners glaze and paint over the dried shapes. Attach to the tops of cakes using royal icing supported in place with a cocktail stick until secure.

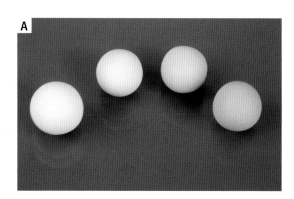
A

Making the garland

1 Select one type of bead and thread a few onto the copper bullion wire (**A**). Hold the last threaded bead in one hand, and the wire, either side of the bead in the other hand and twist the bead onto the wire by rotating it one-and-a-half times. Leave a space, and repeat for the remaining beads on the wire. Check that the garland is long enough to go around the base of the cake then twist the wire ends into the garland so that a bead sits at either end.

2 Create individual garlands for the other types of beads you have chosen (**B**). Arrange the garlands loosely around the base of the cake, interweaving the ends of each so that they are secure.

A

B

Piping champagne bubbles

1 Place a no. 4 tube and some light sepia coloured royal icing into a piping bag. Pipe a few balls on the top and sides of the cake.

2 Continue piping smaller balls with a no. 3 and no. 2 tube to resemble bubbles rising up a champagne glass. If your bubbles are slightly pointed, quickly knock the point back into the bubble with a damp brush before the icing sets.

tip

Check the consistency of the royal icing before you begin piping. You need to be able to pipe bubbles not pointed cones.

Preparing the crown

1 Cut three 15cm (6in) lengths of the copper beading wire. Take a 6mm (¼in) burnt-orange miracle bead and thread it onto of the cut lengths. Using your thumb and index finger of one hand, hold the bead in the middle of the wire then bring the wires together between your thumb and index finger of your other hand so that the bead is locked into position. Twist the bead repeatedly while slowly allowing the wire in your other hand to slide through your fingers to obtain an even twist. Twist the wire until the twist is 5cm (2in) long, then separate the wires to form a T-shape (**C**). Make three.

2 For the coils, cut approximately 25cm (9⅞in) of 0.5mm antique gold coloured craft wire, clasp one end of the wire between round-nosed pliers and wrap the wire around one side of the pliers to create a perfect circle in the wire (**D**).

3 Place the circle horizontally between a pair of flat-nosed pliers and, with your spare hand, push the wire away from you so that it wraps itself partly around the central circle. Reposition the circle and wrap more wire around the circle; you are aiming to wrap about a quarter of the circle before repositioning it (**E**).

4 Repeat until the circle is large enough to hold in your fingers, then, using your fingers, continue coiling the wire until the coil has a diameter of 1.3cm (½in). Measure 3cm (1⅛in) from the coil and bend the wire to create an L-shape. Repeat to make six coils in total.

5 Thread two coil stems and the twist of an amber miracle bead (undo the T-shape) through the hole of a rich-brown wooden bead, then reposition the wires to create the required T-shape (**F**). Repeat to make three groupings.

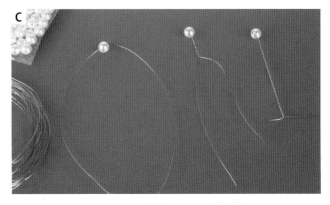

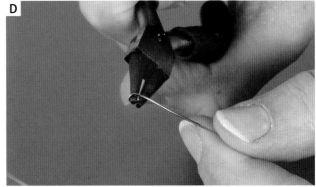

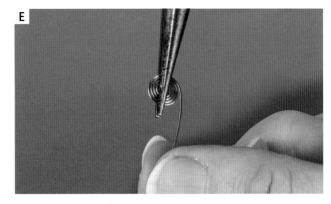

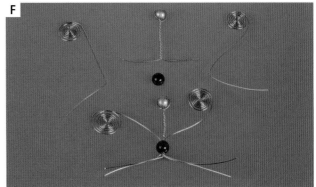

Preparing the crown

1 Cut a short length of the strong jewellery wire and a few lengths of copper beading wire. Starting near one end, hold one of the prepared wire T-shapes onto the strong wire and wrap the beading wire around both wires on one side of the T to bind the two neatly together. Hold the next T so that its twist lies 1cm (³⁄₈in) from the one already secured (**G**).

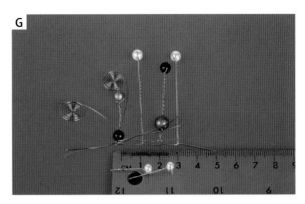

2 Neatly wrap the 0.3mm antique gold coloured craft wire around all three wires between the two twists so that they are all bound securely in place. Continue this process to add the three T-shapes (**H**).

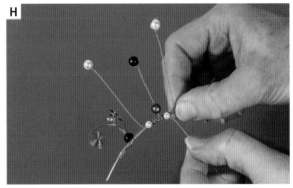

3 To join the crown together, continue binding until you reach the end of the wire, then abut the two ends of the strong wire and continue binding the Ts until you reach your start point. Set aside.

Note: the beaded crown and garland should be removed from the cake before it is carved.

Attaching the crown

If necessary, adjust the shape of the base of the crown to create a circle. Then, pipe royal icing along the underside of the crown. Place the crown centrally on top of the cake. Take a damp paintbrush and neaten any visible royal icing, if necessary. Allow the icing to dry. Once the royal icing that holds the crown in place has set, position and bend the beads and wires as desired.

Eastern Promises

Reproduce the exotic beauty of Indian decoration with these luxurious mini cakes, which are almost too beautiful to eat. The traditional Indian red, burgundy and opulent gold colours combine beautifully with intricate floral, paisley and teardrop motifs to create impressive jewelled miniature 'boxes' that instantly suggest the mysterious East.

These luxurious mini cakes are simple to create and would make a great gift for anyone who loves India, its art and its culture. You could also make them as wedding favours for an Asian wedding celebration or let them spice up a Bollywood themed party.

Although the designs are intricate, they are quick to create using cutters and royal icing piping. The individual designs and colours are easily interchangeable.

you will need …

materials

- sugarpaste (rolled fondant): ivory, burgundy
- white vegetable fat (shortening)
- cakes: 5cm (2in) mulitmini cake pans, multimini hexagonal pans (optional)
- buttercream (see page 19)
- modelling paste: red, gold, cream, ivory, burgundy
- sugar glue (see page 19)
- royal icing
- gold edible dust
- confectioners' glaze
- paste colours: ivory or cream
- sugar balls: 4mm (⅛in) silver, 4mm (⅛in) pearlised gold

equipment

- glass-headed dressmakers' pins
- 5mm (³⁄₁₆in) spacers
- smoother
- palette knife
- narrow spacers made from 1.5mm (¹⁄₁₆in) thick card
- piping tubes (tips): no. 2
- reusable piping bag and coupler
- multi ribbon cutter
- cutters: Indian scrolls and petal set (LC), paisley cutters (LC), small teardrop cutters (LC), small six-petal flower cutter, such as one from flat floral collection set 1 (LC)
- paintbrush
- craft knife
- cutting wheel

Preparing the cakes

1 Bake your cakes in 5cm (2in) multimini cake pans or cut a larger cake into 5cm (2in) deep slices (see pages 12–14). Using a 5cm (2in) circle cutter, cut the slices into rounds. Cut the hexagonal cakes using a 5cm (2in) side-to-side hexagonal cutter or template.

2 Cover the cakes with the burgundy or ivory sugarpaste (see page 17). Leave to dry.

tip

For a completely different look, try creating these little cakes in your favourite colour palette. They look striking in a range of vibrant pinks or cool blues and greens.

Decorating the cakes

Use the techniques below as inspiration to decorate your own cakes as you wish, using a variety of cutters to achieve different effects.

Making the trims

1 Knead the red modelling paste and then roll it out into a long strip between narrow spacers. Take the multi-ribbon cutter and, using one cutting wheel and one wavy-line cutting wheel, set the distance between the two outside edges to 7mm (⁹/₃₂in). Cut strips of red paste (**A**).

2 Indent the strips with the sharp end of a Dresden tool (**B**). Paint sugar glue around the base of the cake and add the textured strips, abutting the ends together.

3 Alternatively, soften some gold modelling paste by kneading in some white vegetable fat and boiled water until it has the consistency of chewing gum. Put into the sugar shaper, with the small round disc, and squeeze out a length. Place the length around the base of the cake. Cut to size and secure with sugar glue.

Creating the paisley decorations

1 Roll out modelling pastes in three colours of
your choice. Cut out small medium and large
paisley shapes from different colours of paste (**C**).

2 Stack the shapes and attach to the cake using
sugar glue. Indent the centre of some with a
pin. Add sugar balls, using royal icing to secure, to
all the circular indentations made in the paste.

3 Dip a fine paintbrush into the sugar glue
and paint around one of the paisley shapes,
extending the point into a scroll. Squeeze out a
length of gold modelling paste from the sugar
shaper fitted with the small round disc. Place the
length over the glue and adjust the scroll. Cut the
paste at the end of a scroll with the tip of a palette
knife. Repeat for the other paisley shapes.

tip

*Sugar balls can tarnish
quickly so add them to the
shapes at the last minute.*

Creating the floral details

1 Thinly roll out the gold modelling paste between the narrow spacers and use the six-petal flat floral cutter to cut out small flowers. Place on waxed paper. Mix the edible gold dust with confectioners' glaze and paint over each one (**D**).

2 Allow the glaze to set for two minutes then remove the centre from each flower with the no. 18 piping tube (**E**). Attach to the mini cake using sugar glue.

Adding the royal icing details

1 Colour the royal icing ivory or a very pale cream. Attach a no. 2 tube to the piping bag using a coupler. Half fill the bag with royal icing and pipe dots on the paisleys. Change the tube to a no. 1 and pipe dots around the shapes and patterns on the cakes (see finished cakes for reference).

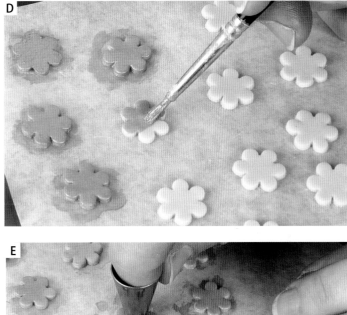

tip

Check the consistency of the royal icing and adjust as necessary, by adding more sugar or boiled water.

Greek Unique

Recreate the symmetry of ancient Greek architecture and design with
this unique trio of mini cakes. The warm, traditional colours of light gold,
terracotta and navy blue are used to create bold triangles and the classical
palmette motif – a fan-shaped ornamental pattern that resembles a palm leaf
and is a symbol of peace. Gold trims and scrolls also add a touch of grandeur.

The cakes are very simple to bake and cover, and by adding simple trims
and motifs, they are soon transformed to capture the essence of Greek art.
They make a perfect bon voyage gift for someone who is moving to the
Mediterranean or anyone who has Greek roots or loves Greece.

*Because most of the decoration is made using cut-out
shapes an essence of Greece is simple to achieve.*

you will need ...

materials

- sugarpaste (rolled fondant): navy blue, light gold
- white vegetable fat (shortening)
- cakes: cut into portions 4cm (1½in) square x 3.5cm (1⅜in) high
- buttercream (see page 19)
- sugar glue (see page 19)
- modelling paste: terracotta, antique gold
- edible dust colours: antique gold (SK)
- confectioners' glaze

equipment

- smoother
- palette knife
- Greek motif embosser – set 2, side designs (HP)
- sugar shaper with small and medium round discs
- paintbrush
- craft knife
- multi ribbon cutter (optional)
- Dresden tool
- piping tube (tip) no. 3
- narrow spacers made from 1.5mm (⅟₁₆in) thick card
- cutters: small teardrop set (LC)
- scriber
- glass-headed dressmakers' pins
- straight edge, such as a ruler

Preparing the cakes

1 Bake your cake (see pages 12–14) and cut into portions 4cm (1½in) square x 3.5cm (1⅜in) high.

2 Cover each portion with light-gold sugarpaste (see page 17). Leave to dry.

tip

Use Spectral colours autumn leaf to make a gold-coloured paste.

Adding the trim

Creating the gold embossed band

1 Soften some gold modelling paste by firstly kneading in some white vegetable fat to stop the paste getting sticky and then partially dunking the paste into a small container of boiled water before kneading again. Place the softened paste with the medium round disc into the sugar shaper.

2 Take a fine paintbrush and, using some sugar glue, paint a line of glue around the base of the cake. Squeeze out a long length of paste from the shaper and carefully place it around the base of the cake. Cut one end at 45 degrees, using a craft knife, then cut the other end also at 45 degrees so that the two ends will sit snugly together. Glue the ends together using sugar glue and blend the join neatly with the wide end of a Dresden tool.

3 Take a no. 3 piping tube and press it repeatedly into the trim to create a textured finish.

Creating the navy-blue embossed border

1 Knead the navy-blue sugarpaste to warm it. Use a craft knife and straight edge or a multi ribbon cutter to cut the sugarpaste to a suitable length to wrap around the cake.

2 Press the Greek motif embosser at one end into the soft paste. Line up the embosser so that the next embossed shape will be adjacent to the first, and press down. Repeat until you have embossed the entire length of sugarpaste.

3 Take a fine paintbrush and, using some sugar glue, paint a line of glue around the base of the cake. Carefully place the embossed trim over the sugar glue.

4 Paint a thin line of sugar glue around the top of the navy blue trim. Soften some of the antique-gold modelling paste, place in the sugar shaper with the small round disc and squeeze out a length. Attach to the sugar glue to add a band around the top of your trim.

tip

For best results, the paste should have the consistency of chewing gum.

Decorating the cakes

Use these techniques as inspiration to decorate your own cakes as you wish, using a
variety of cutters and tools to achieve different effects.

Creating the gold scrolls

1 Draw a scroll pattern onto tracing or greaseproof
paper, using the picture for reference. Place the
prepared paper across two sides of the cake, secure in
place with a few pins, then carefully scribe the pattern
onto the cake by going over the pencil lines with
either a scriber or a pin. Remove all the pins and the
template, and repeat for the opposite two sides.

2 Dip a fine paintbrush into the sugar glue then
paint over each scroll (**A**).

3 Soften some of the antique-gold modelling paste.
Place in the sugar shaper with the small round disc
and squeeze out a length (shown here on a larger cake
design) (**B**). Place the length of paste over one of the
painted glue scrolls and adjust its shape with a finger
and/or a paintbrush. Cut the paste neatly at either end
of the scroll with the tip of a small palette knife. Repeat
for the remaining scroll.

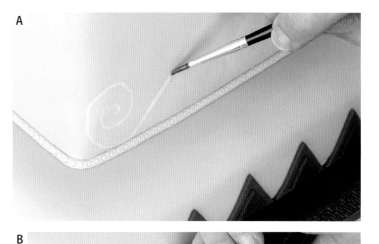

A

B

tip

*If the paste does not come
out easily it is still too hard,
so remove and re-soften.*

Creating the palmette motif

1 Thinly roll out some terracotta modelling paste between narrow spacers. Using the small teardrop cutter set, cut shapes as shown. Repeat with the navy-blue modelling paste. Then cut a number of small triangles.

2 Arrange the cut-outs on your work board to resemble a radiating cluster of petals (right). Gently curve all but the central teardrop by fractionally reshaping the paste (**C**).

3 Using sugar glue, stick the navy-blue triangles in position on the top of the cake. Finally, cut out a circle from the antique gold modelling paste using an appropriately sized piping tube, and attach to the centre of the motif (**D**).

Creating the top tile decoration

1 Thinly roll out some navy-blue modelling paste and cut out a small square. Attach this to the cake using sugar glue.

2 Thinly roll out some terracotta and antique gold modelling paste. Use the smallest cutters from the small teardrop set to cut out four shapes from each cutter.

3 Arrange into a star shape, referring to the picture, and attach to the navy-blue square of modelling paste using sugar glue. Add a gold trim using the technique described for the gold embossed band (see page 75).

C

D

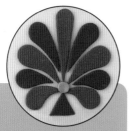

tip

Mix some edible antique gold dust with confectioners' glaze and use to paint over all the decorations made from the antique-gold modelling paste.

Lovely Lilies

Elegant and beautiful, arum lilies were often used as motifs in Art Nouveau decoration, and today these sculptural blooms are becoming especially popular as bridal flowers. These gorgeous mini cakes capture the beauty and simplicity of Art Nouveau design, with its soft curves and contrasting straight lines, combined here with realistic flowers made from flower paste.

These mini cakes make exquisite wedding favours, as the ivory and cream shades perfectly complement a bridal colour scheme. They would also bring a feminine touch to a birthday celebration, or could even be given to celebrate an anniversary or engagement – perfect because the lilies are in pairs.

You can achieve the beautifully crafted lilies by using a cutter and delicately tinting the flowers with edible dusts.

you will need …

materials

- sugarpaste (rolled fondant): cream, white
- white vegetable fat (shortening)
- cakes: 5cm (2in) mulitmini cake pans (optional)
- sugar glue (page 19)
- modelling pastes: gold (colour to match edible gold dust), deep yellow, cream, white, green
- semolina
- edible dust colours: light-gold lustre dust (SK)
- buttercream (see page 19)
- white flower paste (petal/gum paste)
- confectioners' glaze

equipment

- 5cm (2in) cake boards
- 5cm (2in) circle cutter
- small arum lily cutter (LC)
- smoother
- straight edge
- sugar shaper with medium and small round discs
- Dresden tool
- 5mm (³⁄₁₆in) spacers – made from thick card
- scriber (optional)
- craft knife
- foam pad
- ball tool
- selection of brushes, including a dusting brush
- baking paper or tracing paper
- small scissors
- cutting wheel

Preparing the cakes

1 Bake your cakes in 5cm (2in) multimini cake pans or cut a larger cake into 5cm (2in) deep slices (see pages 12–14). Using a 5cm (2in) circle cutter, cut the slices into rounds.

2 Level the mini cakes. Place the cakes individually on the 5cm (2in) hardboard cake boards, securing the boards in place with buttercream. Spread a thin layer of buttercream over the cake to stick the sugarpaste. Knead some white sugarpaste to warm it, then roll out between the 5mm (³⁄₁₆in) spacers. Cut out 5cm (2in) circles using the cutter and place a circle of paste over the top of each cake.

3 Roll out more white sugarpaste into a long strip. Turn the paste over and cut it into a 5cm (2in) wide long rectangle. Place a cake on its side onto the paste so the covered top is flush with one long edge. Roll up the cake in the paste (shown in the picture on a larger cake design – **A**). Trim as necessary to create a neat straight join and rub closed, the heat from your hand should make the join disappear but if not it can easily be disguised by the decoration. Stand the cake upright on waxed paper and allow to dry.

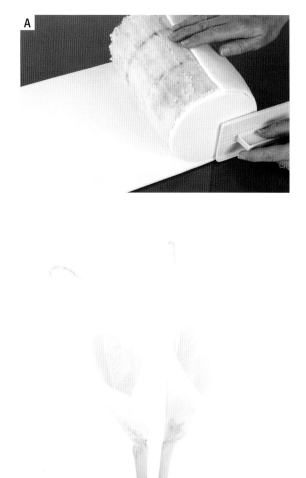
A

Decorating the cakes

Start by thinly rolling out the white modelling paste and cutting out 5cm (2in) circles. Place a circle over the top of each cake to help neaten its appearance.

Attaching the cream decoration

1 Make a paper template for the cream decoration by cutting stripes of baking or tracing paper to fit around your cakes. Using a pencil, draw a suitable wavy line pattern onto the paper referring to the pictures for guidance. Cut along the line with sharp scissors to make your template.

2 Roll out the cream modelling paste between the narrow spacers, ensuring that it is large enough to fit the template. Cut one long edge straight then place the template over the paste aligning the cut edge. Next cut around the template with a cutting wheel or craft knife. Paint sugar glue over the underside of the cream paste and carefully attach it to the sides of a cake ensuring the straight edge is flush with the base.

3 Place some softened cream modelling paste in the sugar shaper with the small round disc. Paint sugar glue along the cut edge of the cream modelling paste added earlier. Squeeze out a length and position over the glue (**B**). Cut to fit.

B

tip

To soften the paste, first knead in some white vegetable fat to stop it getting sticky, then partially dunk into a small container of boiled water before kneading again.

Adding gold vertical line and scroll decorations

1 Place some softened gold modelling paste inside the sugar shaper with the small round disc. Paint a vertical line of sugar glue onto each cake. Squeeze out the paste over the glue. Trim to fit and use a straightedge to adjust if necessary.

2 Use a craft knife to cut the scrolls freehand from thinly rolled gold modelling paste. Attach with sugar glue.

Creating the lilies

1 Smear white fat over your work board, and then thinly roll out some white flower paste. Cut out two lilies for each cake using the arum lily cutter.

2 Place the paste onto the foam pad. Use the ball tool to stroke around the edges of the paste by pressing the tool half on the paste and half on the pad to soften the edge (**C**).

3 Press a cocktail stick repeatedly into the centre of the paste to create a radial pattern (**D**).

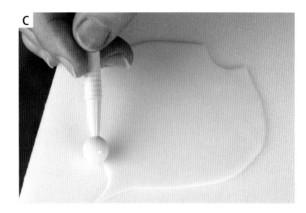

C

D

Making the lily centres

1 For the lily centres (spadices), roll the deep-yellow modelling paste into two small sausage shapes. Put some semolina in a small plastic bag and add some deep-yellow edible dust. Shake the bag to colour the semolina. Add more colour if necessary and shake again. Cover a spadix with sugar glue, pop it into the bag of semolina and shake to cover. Remove and repeat for the other spadices (**E**).

2 Take a spadice and place it in position at the base of the spathe. Pick up the sides of the spathes and wrap them around the spadix, securing with sugar glue. Gently encourage the edges of the spathe to curl slightly outwards (**F**).

3 Using a soft brush, dust the centre of each lily with deep-yellow dust (**G**). Place the completed lilies directly in position on the cake using a little sugar glue to secure. Leave to dry.

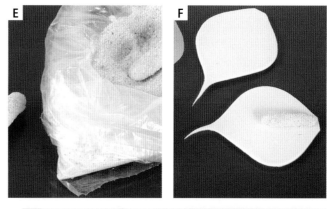

Creating the stems

1 Place some softened green modelling paste in the sugar shaper with the medium disc. Paint glue where the stems will rest on the cake. Squeeze out lengths of paste and place them over the glue. Cut to fit.

2 Blend the stem into the flower with a Dresden tool. Mix some green dust with clear spirit and paint over the tip of each flower, the stem and the back of the spathe.

tip

To gild the decorations, mix the light gold lustre dust with confectioners' glaze and paint over the gold scrolls and the vertical lines.

Rustic Leaves

Reminiscent of 1970s' design, these curled leaf creations capture the end of summer with their golden and red hues and their mass of swirling patterns, creating a real sense of movement. The interesting pyramid shapes are simply formed by carving round cakes to shape and most of the details can be added using cutters, embossers or texturing tools.

The real beauty of these mini cakes is the versatility of designs to be made. By following and adapting the general instructions overleaf, you can make each design truly unique. They would make an eye-catching retirement gift or could be given as unusual favours for a seasonal wedding.

Bold, rustic colours combine with interesting three-dimensional textures for a stunning effect.

you will need ...

materials

- sugarpaste (rolled fondant): light-peach
- white vegetable fat (shortening)
- cakes: 5cm (2in) mulitmini cake pans (optional)
- buttercream (see page 19)
- clear spirit, such as gin or vodka
- sugar glue (see page 19)

- modelling pastes in a selection of colours: e.g. brown, yellow, gold, light orange, red, dark orange, yellow-brown, ruby red, black, dark red, olive, light green, dark olive, light peach

equipment

- 5mm (³⁄₁₆in) spacers
- smoother
- palette knife
- scriber
- cutting wheel
- narrow spacers made from 1.5mm (¹⁄₁₆in) thick card
- sugar shaper with fine mesh, small and medium round discs
- Dresden tool
- ball tool
- piping tubes (tips) no. 18 (PME)

- mini embossers: e.g. curved zigzag (HP set 3, border designs), floral motif (HP set 2, side design), small flowers (HP set 1, small floral), grapes (HP set 11, vine and berry)
- craft knife
- pan scourer (new)
- fluting tool (JEM),
- cutters: circle cutters: 2.5cm (1in) and 2.1cm (²⁷⁄₃₂in) circles, five-petal flower from flat floral collection set 1 (LC), large blossom set (FMM)
- daisy centre stamps (JEM)

Preparing the cakes

1 Bake your cakes in 5cm (2in) multimini cake pans or alternatively cut a larger cake into 5cm (2in) deep slices (see pages 12–14) and then, using a 5cm (2in) circle cutter, cut the slices into rounds.

2 Mark the centre of the cakes with a cocktail stick, then take a large carving knife and cut down from the cocktail stick to the bottom of the cakes to create cone shapes. Remove a little cake at a time and stand back from the cake occasionally to check that your cone is symmetrical. Place the cakes on waxed paper.

3 Using greaseproof paper, make a template for the sugarpaste by holding one edge of the paper vertically against the side of the cake while wrapping the paper around the cake. Cut the paper vertically so that the two straight edges meet. Trim the excess from the base. You should have a circular segment slightly larger than quarter of a circle.

tip

You will find it easier to carve your cakes whilst frozen, so freeze them for a few hours before carving.

4 Knead and roll out the sugarpaste between the 5mm (³/₁₆in) spacers to fit the template. Place the template on the paste and cut around it with a palette knife.

5 Place the paste on your rolling pin with the curved outside edge of the segment hanging over one side and the tip/centre of the segment over the other. Position the curved edge at the base of the cake and carefully unroll the pin upwards to position the paste onto the cone. Using your hand and a smoother, position the cut sides of the paste so that they meet. Trim away the excess at the join with scissors and blend with a smoother. Leave to dry.

tip

If the join in your sugarpaste doesn't disappear, the leaf decoration can be positioned to cover any visible join.

Decorating the cakes

The decorated leaf designs on these cakes can be made as simple or detailed as you desire using different coloured sugarpaste and a selection of cutters and tools. Here, I am giving you some basic instructions about how to create certain elements that make up these three mini cakes to inspire you to create your own unique design.

It may be useful for you to draw your chosen pattern onto tracing or greaseproof paper before starting, then pin your tracing to the cake and scribe the design onto the cake before you begin. Roll out each modelling paste between narrow spacers and attach each completed section onto the cake using sugar glue.

Adding texture to the modelling paste

1 Create dimples in the paste by pressing the small end of the ball tool repeatedly into the paste (**A**).

2 For a zig-zag pattern, press the curved zigzag embosser repeatedly around the edge of the shape (**B**). For a floral design, emboss in the same way using the mini floral motif embosser.

3 To give your modelling paste a rough texture, press a pan scourer repeatedly into the surface of your paste (**C**).

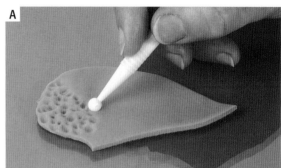

tip

Add an extra dimension to your design by rolling up pea-sized balls of paste in a contrasting colour and attaching in a random pattern.

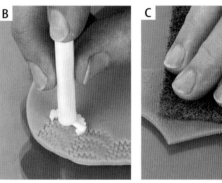

Adding the three-dimensional paste strands

1 Soften some gold modelling paste by kneading in some white vegetable fat and boiled water until the consistency of chewing gum. Place in the sugar shaper with the fine mesh disc.

2 Paint over the section that you want to apply the strands to with sugar glue. Squeeze out short lengths of paste, removing them from the sugar shaper with the end of a Dresden tool, and attach them to the glued area (**D**).

Creating the concentric circles

1 Cut out dark-red circles using the wide end of a piping tube and yellow circles using a no. 18 tube, or use appropriately sized cutters for different sized circles. Place the yellow circles on top of the red and attach, equally spaced, within the red border.

2 Insert the pointed end of the fluting tool into the centre of each set of circles to reveal the red paste underneath.

3 Alternatively, remove smaller off-centre circles from each of your sugarpaste circles using the no. 18 piping tube (**E**). Attach to the cake using sugar glue.

Creating floral design

1 Cut out a black circle and a red and light-orange five-petal blossom from sugarpaste. Place a smoother on top of the red blossom and press hard to flatten the paste and enlarge the flower.

2 Place the red blossom and then the orange one on top of the black circle, and cut out the centre using the 1.3cm (½in) wide daisy centre stamp (only remove the red and orange paste, not the black) (**F**). Attach to the cake using sugar glue.

Adding trims

Put some softened black modelling paste in the sugar shaper with the medium round disc. Paint glue in the position that you want to place the trim. Squeeze out a length of paste and position over the glue. Cut to fit with a craft knife and texture with the Dresden tool.

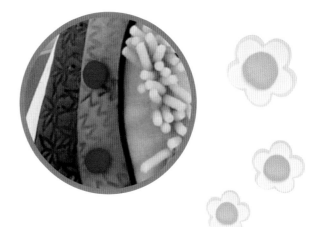

Funky Fish

The Art Nouveau mosaics of Catalan architect Antoni Gaudi (1852–1926) were the inspiration for this truly unique collection. Intricate mosaic designs adorn each mini cake – each tessera carefully added by hand. Silvery fish are simply created using wire or sugarpaste and look striking swimming across the smooth surfaces or springing from the top of the cakes.

These delicate mini cakes would make a spectacular gift for someone who loves mosaic art from the Mediterranean or who appreciates the unusual. The aquatic blues look clean against the crisp white of the sugarpaste and give a hint of sunlit pools that is guaranteed to brighten up your day.

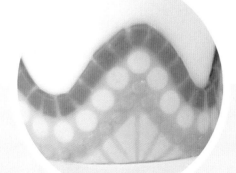

Each tessera is individually cut from sugarpaste then attached to the sides of the cake with sugar glue. The mosaic design may appear fiddly, but the effect is not difficult to reproduce – just take your time.

you will need ...

materials

- sugarpaste (rolled fondant): mid blue, white, pale blue
- cakes: 5cm (2in) mulitmini cake pans (optional)
- modelling paste: different shades of blue; white, grey
- white vegetable fat
- sugar glue (see page 19)

- buttercream (see page 19) or apricot glaze and marzipan (see page 16)
- clear spirit, such as gin or vodka
- edible snowflake lustre dust

equipment

- narrow spacers made from 1.5mm (¹⁄₁₆in) thick card
- set square
- craft knife
- paintbrushes
- palette knife
- piping tubes (tips) no.s 18, 17, 16, 4 (PME)

- 1.5mm (16/17g SWG/15g AWG) aluminium wire
- round-nosed pliers
- wire cutters
- smoother
- posy pick
- oasis fix

Preparing the cakes

1 Bake your cakes in 5cm (2in) multimini cake pans or cut a larger cake into 5cm (2in) deep slices, and then use a 5cm (2in) circle cutter to cut the slices into rounds.

2 Cover the cakes with the white sugarpaste (see page 17). Leave to dry.

tip

Try adding a little white fat and/or boiled water to soften the modelling paste before kneading it.

Decorating the cakes

Use the following techniques as inspiration to decorate your own mini cakes.

Adding the tiles

1 Knead modelling paste in various shades of blue to warm it. Roll the paste out between narrow spacers.

2 Use a set square and a craft knife to cut out squares or use the wide end of one of the piping tubes to create circles (**A**). Triangles, or any other shape of your choice, can also be cut out using a set square and craft knife or appropriate cutters.

3 Use sugar glue to paint wave shapes on the sides of the cake. Lift and separate some of the mosaic tiles using a palette knife. Using a damp brush, place the tiles onto the sugar glue wave, leaving a small gap between each tile (**B**). To achieve a close fit on the sharper curves remove a narrow tapered triangle from some of the squares when in place. Continue adding rows of tiles, changing colour and shape with each row. Leave to dry.

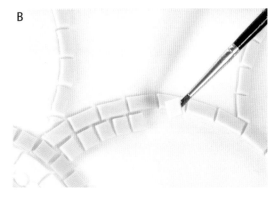

4 To 'grout' the tiles, knead some light-blue sugarpaste, add boiled water and blend with a palette knife until it becomes a soft spreadable consistency. Working in sections, spread the softened sugarpaste over some of the dried tiles so that the paste fills all the gaps between the tiles. Remove as much excess paste as possible using a palette knife then use a folded, dampened paper towel to carefully remove all the remaining paste from the surface of the tiles (**C**).

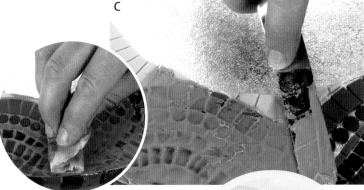

Adding the tile trims

1 To add a tile trim to the base of your mini cake, cut squares of dark blue modelling paste. Glue the dark blue squares in a ring around the base. Create a circle tile topper by adding a small circle and then a ring of squares, cutting the squares to fit as necessary on the cakes. Allow to dry.

Making the wire topper

1 Cut a length of aluminium wire. Clasp one end of the wire between round-nosed pliers and wrap the wire around one side of the pliers to create a circle in the wire (**D**).

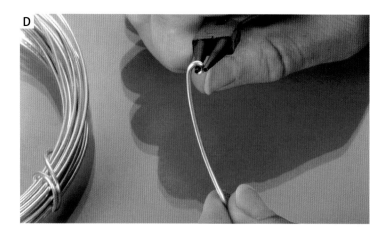

D

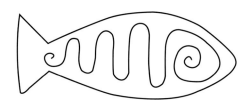

2 Place the wire circle over the fish's eye on the template above. Press down on the eye with the finger of one hand while bending the wire to shape following the lines of the template with your other hand (**E**). Reposition the finger that is pressing down on the wire as necessary. Once complete, bring the remaining length of the wire over to form a loop and then down below the fish. Repeat to form the second fish.

3 Insert a posy pick vertically into the centre of the cake with its surface fractionally below the surface of the sugarpaste. Place a small amount of oasis fix into the posy pick to help secure the wires. Take a wire fish and gently create a wave in the wire. Cut to an appropriate length and insert into the posy pick. Repeat.

E

Creating the sugar fish

1 Place some clear plastic over the fish template (opposite) and trace onto the plastic using a pencil. Cut around the traced lines with a small pair of scissors.

2 Roll out some white modelling paste. Place the template onto the paste and cut around it with a craft knife (**F**).

3 Take your wire topper (see page 94) and position it over one of the cut-out paste fish. Press down firmly so the wire indents the paste (**G**).

4 Soften some grey modelling paste by kneading it in some white vegetable fat and boiled water. Put the paste in the sugar shaper with the small round disc. With a fine paintbrush, paint a line of sugar glue into the indented areas of the fish.

4 Squeeze out some paste and place the end into the eye of the fish; continue squeezing and positioning the paste until the fish is complete (**H**).

5 Dust the fish with snowflake lustre dust. Using sugar glue, attach the finished fish to the side of your cake (**I**).

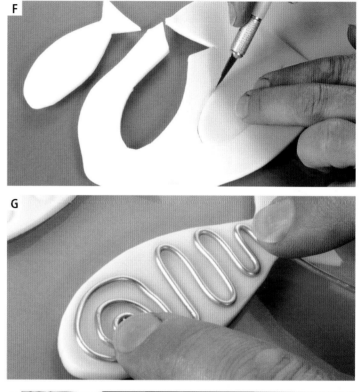

Children's

Baby Blocks

This delightful collection of decorated pastel-coloured bricks is child's play to create. Go to town with your decorative motifs and use a selection of cutter designs to either emboss each square or add as cut-outs for that extra dimension. What makes the cakes so striking is that each side of the cube is bordered with a different coloured paste – a simple but professional touch.

These baby-sized bricks would make a fantastic gift for a baby shower, a christening party or simply to treat a new mum. They are perfect for a baby's first or second birthday party, or you can adapt the design for an older child by using bolder colours and choosing suitable decorations such as space ships, flowers or cut-out fairies.

Decorate each side of the cube using a variety of patchwork cutters, such as polar bears, ducks, teddy bears, blocks and butterflies.

you will need . . .

materials

- sugarpaste (rolled fondant): orange, yellow, purple, lilac, light pink, coral pink, dark pink, lime green, light aqua, mid blue
- icing (confectioners') sugar (optional)
- white vegetable fat (shortening)
- cakes: 5cm (2in) cube portions
- buttercream (see page 19)
- gum tragacanth
- sugar glue (see page 19)

equipment

- smoother
- palette knife
- set square
- patchwork cutters, e.g. baby lion and nursery items set (feet and bow), butterflies, polar bear set, daisy chain, make a cradle (teddy), nursery set (blocks)
- narrow spacers made from 1.5mm (¹⁄₁₆in) thick card
- multi-ribbon cutter (FMM)
- craft knife
- cutters: flat floral collection sets 1 and 2 (LC) or similar, elegant hearts (LC) or similar

Preparing the cakes

1 Cut a cake (see pages 12–14) into 5cm (2in) cube portions, by using a sharp knife. Level the top of the cake, then adjust the sides so that they are all vertical and the corners square (**A**).

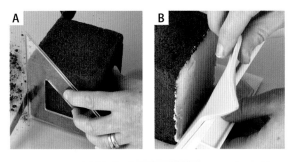

2 Spread buttercream over one side of the cake. Knead the orange sugarpaste until warm and roll out. Cut one edge straight, using a palette knife. Lift up the sugarpaste and position it over the buttercreamed side of the cake, placing the straight edge against the lower edge of the cake (**B**).

3 Smooth the paste to give an even surface then roughly cut away the excess paste with a pair of scissors. Place the smoother onto the surface then, using a palette knife, remove the excess paste by cutting away from the cake onto the smoother (**C**).

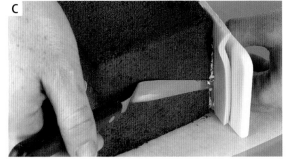

4 Take a cutter design of your choice, press it centrally into the soft sugarpaste and remove to leave an embossed shape (**D**). Cover the opposite side of the cube in the same way, using a different colour and cutter.

5 For the next side, roll out a different colour of sugarpaste, cut one edge straight then make a cut at right angles. Position on the cake as for the first side, so that the edge abuts one side of the orange square (**D**). Trim as before then straighten the corner with a smoother. Repeat for the remaining sides and top of the cake, using a different coloured paste. For the top of the cake, you will need to cut upwards against the smoother.

6 Cover the remaining cakes with the different-coloured sugarpastes (**E**), embossing some of the sides with cutters of your choice. These remaining sides can either be left blank or decorated by cutting shapes from thinly rolled modelling paste and attaching to the cakes using sugar glue.

Adding border decoration

1 Make modelling paste by taking 50g (2oz) of each of the coloured sugarpastes and kneading in 1.5ml (¼ tsp) gum tragacanth to each colour. Leave the paste to mature, ideally overnight.

2 Choose a colour of modelling paste and knead the paste to warm it. Roll out the paste between the narrow spacers. Set the multi-ribbon cutter to a width of 8mm (5⁄16in) then use to cut ribbons (**F**).

3 Paint glue along the vertical cut edges of the sugarpaste on one side of a cube and position the strips on top of the glue to disguise the cut edges. Check that the strips are vertical using a set square then cut to fit with a craft knife (**G**). Cut more strips with the multiribbon cutter in different colours, and use to disguise the edges of the paste on all of the bricks, each time cutting to fit with a craft knife.

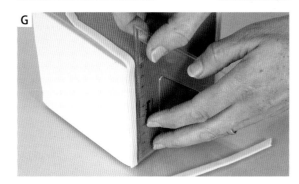

tip

If the paste is either a bit hard or too crumbly add a little white fat and/or boiled water to soften. It should be firm with some elasticity. Alternatively place the paste in a microwave for a few seconds to soften.

Happy Hedgehog

He might be covered in prickles but this gorgeous garden visitor would be a most welcome guest at any party. Chocolate cake is baked in a shaped pan and then covered with dark chocolate buttercream for this straightforward cake. The delicious prickles are made from flavoured chocolate sticks and sugarpaste features are added to create an endearing face that gives the hedgehog an irresistible appearance.

Apart from making a great cake for a child's birthday, this spiky hedgehog would be a fun choice for a gardener's birthday or to treat a wildlife enthusiast. Or why not make up a whole family of hedgehogs in different sizes to really impress your guests?

The spikes are easily created by adding mint or orange-flavoured chocolate sticks, however these can be substituted for chocolate buttons, flakes or finger biscuits if you prefer.

you will need ...

materials

- half-ball shaped mini cakes
- chocolate buttercream
- paste colours: golden brown (Spectral Autumn Leaf), dark brown
- sugarpaste (rolled fondant): ivory or white, brown
- mint- or orange-flavoured chocolate sticks
- icing sugar (optional)
- white vegetable fat
- modelling paste: white, black, golden brown
- sugar glue

equipment

- 5mm (³/₁₆in) spacers
- 18cm (7in) cake boards
- mini-ball or Mini-wonder Mold cake pans (W) or 10cm (4in) ball tin
- smoother
- palette knife
- oval cutters

Preparing the cakes

1 Using the golden-brown paste colour, colour the ivory or white sugarpaste five shades of golden brown. Break the coloured paste into small pieces and scatter them over your work surface to mix up the colours. Gather the scattered pieces together into a ball and briefly knead together. Cut across the ball to reveal the marbled pattern inside.

2 Place the two halves next to one another and then roll the paste out between the 5mm (³/₁₆in) spacers using icing sugar or white vegetable fat to prevent sticking (**A**). Lift up the paste, using a rolling pin for support, and place it over the cake board. Take a smoother and, using a circular motion, smooth the paste to give a level surface. Using a palette knife, trim the edges flush with the sides of the board, taking care to keep the cut vertical. Place to one side to dry.

A

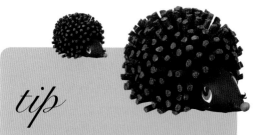

tip

The direction in which you roll the paste will affect the resulting marbled pattern, so try altering the direction you are rolling as the pattern develops.

Decorating the cakes

1 Bake half-ball-shaped mini cakes (see pages 12–14) using one of the suggested tins. Working on one cake at a time, place a cake onto a covered cake board and cover with dark brown chocolate buttercream. Roll 75g (3oz) of brown sugarpaste into a ball and then a cone. Slightly hollow out the wider end with your thumb and stick to your mini cake for a head.

2 Take 300g (11oz) of mint-or orange-flavoured chocolate sticks and break them into pieces, the largest approximately 4cm (1½in) long. Insert the sticks into the cake and leave to dry in place.

Making the faces

1 **For the eyes,** individually roll out some of the white, golden-brown and black modelling paste. Cut two appropriately sized ovals from each colour of modelling paste. Place the golden-brown and black ovals at one end of the larger white ovals and cut away the excess with the largest oval cutter (**B**). Cut two small white triangles and add to the top of each eye for a light spot. Attach in place on the cake using sugar glue to secure.

2 **For the whiskers and eyelashes,** roll out the black modelling paste between the narrow spacers, then take the cutting wheel and run it backwards and forwards through the paste to create long, thin triangles (**C**). Cut across the base of the triangles, arrange two or three on either side of the snout and secure in place with sugar glue (**D**). Support with a pin until dry. Attach two smaller triangles to the corner of each eye for the lashes, and turn the ends up slightly to curve.

3 **For the nose**, knead a small amount of golden-brown modelling paste until warm, adding a little white vegetable fat and boiled water to soften if necessary. Then roll the paste into a ball and attach to the tip of the cake.

Cheeky Monkeys

These mischievous-looking chimps would make great table centrepieces. They each have a broad grin and a twinkle in their eye, and they look full of fun. Use sugarpaste to build up the features and personalize the cakes. The realistic-looking fur is simply made by marking the brown sugarpaste with a cutting tool and then painting over with paste colour.

Invite these little monkeys to any child's party, or make them for a fun-loving adult. If monkeys are not your favourite animals, why not get creative and adapt the modelling techniques to create a variety of animal designs, such as the happy giraffes on page 111? They make perfect party presents and are sure to appeal to your little wild ones.

I have added a trendy baseball cap for a cheeky boy and pretty pink flower for a mischievous girl, however you can add a variety of decorations to suit your own little monkeys.

you will need ...

materials

- small half-ball shaped cakes
- buttercream
- sugarpaste (rolled fondant): white, dark brown, orange-beige
- gum tragacanth
- modelling paste: white, black
- sugar glue

equipment

- greaseproof paper
- half-ball-shaped mini cake pans or 10cm (4in) ball tin
- 5mm (³⁄₁₆in) spacers
- smoother
- palette knife
- Dresden tool
- cutting wheel
- craft knife
- ball tool
- narrow spacers made from 1.5mm (¹⁄₁₆in) thick card
- small oval cutters (LC)
- sugar shaper with small round disc (optional)

Preparing the cakes

1 Bake small half-ball-shaped cakes using the half-ball mini cake pans (W) or the two halves of a 10cm (4in) ball tin (see pages 12–14). Cover the cakes with buttercream.

2 Create eyebrows by taking white sugarpaste, rolling it into a sausage and then attaching it in place onto the front of the face, bringing the ends slightly down the sides of the face (shown here on a larger cake) (**A**).

3 Make the mouth area rounded by adding white sugarpaste to give extra height and shape. Finally, add a cone-shaped piece of white sugarpaste onto the centre of the face for the nose, and smooth the sides (**B**).

Covering the cakes

1 Spread a thin layer of buttercream over the top and
   sides of the head where you want the hair to be
positioned. Knead the dark brown sugarpaste and roll out
between the 5mm (³/₁₆in) spacers. Place the paste over the
section of the head to be covered. Take the smoother and,
whilst pressing down, run the flat edge around the base
of the cake to create a cutting line, and then cut away the
excess paste with a palette knife.

2 Run the cutting wheel repeatedly over the surface of
   the paste to create hair texture, being careful not to
cut right through the paste (**C**).

3 Spread a thin layer of buttercream over the remaining
   cake. Knead the orange-beige sugarpaste and roll it
out between the 5mm (³/₁₆in) spacers. Pick up the paste and
place over the mouth and eye section of the head. Carefully
smooth the paste under the chin making sure there are no
pleats. Cut the excess paste away from the base of the cake
and around the face with a palette knife or craft knife (**D**).
Rub a finger over the cut edge to round it.

4 Take a palette knife and mark four short lines on the
   bridge of the nose, and then insert the small end of a
ball tool into the end of the nose to form nostrils. Extend
each nostril to the side by using the more rounded end of
the Dresden tool (**E**).

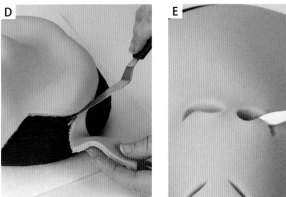

Adding the features

Eyes

1 Individually roll out the white and black modelling
paste between the narrow spacers. Take the oval cutter
and cut out two ovals of each colour. Carefully pick up the
two white ovals and place vertically in position on the face.
Reduce the height of the remaining black ovals by taking
the oval cutter and making another cut (**F**).

2 Attach a foreshortened oval at the base of each eye
to form the pupils. Make light spots by cutting a small
strip from thinly rolled white modelling paste and curving
them slightly. Attach to the eyes so that they lie partly over
the pupil and partly over the whites.

Ears

1 Take 50g (1¾oz) of the orange-beige sugarpaste
trimmings and knead in 1.25ml (¼ tsp) gum tragacanth
to make modelling paste. Leave the paste to mature,
ideally overnight.

2 Roll out the orange-beige modelling paste between
the 5mm (³⁄₁₆in) spacers. Make an ear template of an
appropriate size from greaseproof paper and place it over
the paste. Take a cutting wheel and cut around the template,
then lightly roll the smaller wheel over the C-shaped line
inside the ear. Remove the template and emphasise the C-
shape marking with the sharper end of the Dresden tool (**G**).

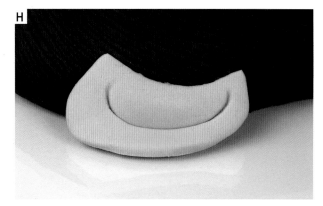

3 Paint some sugar glue along the inside edge of the ear
and attach the ear to the side of the head, so that it
partially rests against the side of the cake (**H**). Repeat for the
second ear.

Mouth

1 Soften some black modelling paste. Place the softened paste with the small round disc into the sugar shaper and squeeze out a length. Take a fine paintbrush, and, using some sugar glue, paint a smile onto the mouth area of the cake.

2 Carefully pick up the length of black paste and place over the painted glue mouth, cut the ends to size with a craft knife. Paint on the corners of the mouth with sugar glue and add small lengths of black paste, again cutting them to size with a craft knife.

Hair

Dilute some brown paste colour in clear spirit and paint over the top and sides of the chimp head's to highlight his hair.

tip

Alternatively, you can roll a very thin piece of modelling paste for the mouth.

Animal magic

Have fun adapting the modelling techniques used here to create a variety of fabulous animal faces, including this friendly pair of giraffes.

Bake oval-shaped bitesized cakes using egg mini cake pans (W) (see pages 12–14). Cover the cakes with buttercream and then cream-coloured sugarpaste (see page 17), and add the features using modelling paste and small cutters.

Little Mermaid

Delight your child or teenager with this beautifully modelled mermaid, happily resting on a rock watching the tide come in. The surface of the rock and fish-scale texture of the mermaid's tail add to the naturalistic appearance of the cake and are easy to achieve. The mermaid's simple features would appeal to any little girl and adding pearlized pale green dragées gives the cake a sparkling finishing touch.

This would make a fantastic birthday cake for your very own little mermaid or water baby. Give yourself plenty of time to create the face and hands, and colour the eyes and hair the same as the person you are making the cake for.

If you are short of time, you can simply create the mermaid topper to embellish a simple covered sponge.

you will need ...

materials

- Madeira cake baked in a small oven proof bowl
- buttercream
- sugarpaste (rolled fondant): white
- modelling paste: flesh, cream, orange, sea green, golden brown, light green
- sugar glue (see page 19)

- paste colours: brown, orange, cream, black
- edible dusts: skin tone/pink for cheeks, green lustre, blue lustre
- sugar stick or uncooked dried spaghetti
- clear spirit, such as gin or vodka
- pearlized pale green dragées (sugar balls)
- white vegetable fat (shortening)

equipment

- Dresden tool
- stippling brush
- selection of round piping tubes (tips)
- narrow spacers made from 1.5mm (¹⁄₁₆in) thick card

- shell mould
- cutting wheel
- foam
- sugar shaper with mesh disc
- ceramic veining tool (HP) or cocktail stick (toothpick)

Creating the rock

1 Level a bowl cake (see page 12) and remove the crusts. Cover the cake with a thin layer of buttercream. Take small pieces of white sugarpaste and add them to the cake to disguise the dome shape and make it look more rocky (**A**).

2 Colour the remaining white sugarpaste a variety of shades of brown and grey. Roughly knead these together then cut the paste in half to reveal the marbled pattern inside. Place the two halves next to each other, cut-side uppermost, and rub the join closed. Roll out the paste and use to cover the cake (**B**).

A
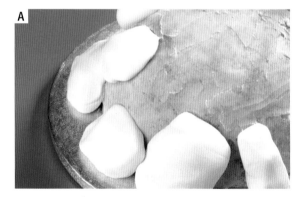

B
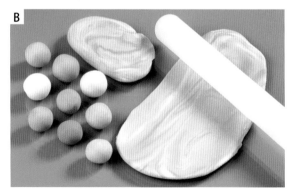

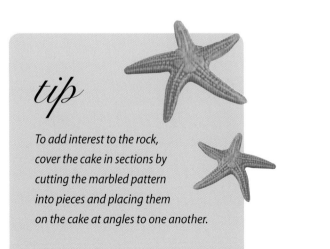

tip

To add interest to the rock, cover the cake in sections by cutting the marbled pattern into pieces and placing them on the cake at angles to one another.

3 To form the rocks, take the sharper end of a Dresden tool and press and drag it through the paste along and across the lines of the marbling (**C**). Roll small balls of sugarpaste and shape into pebbles. Place these randomly in some of the rock crevices.

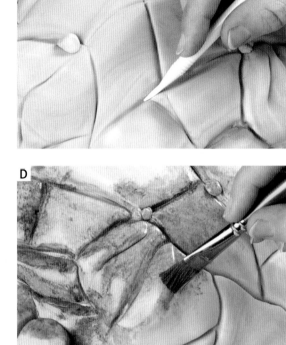

4 Dilute some brown paste colour in clear spirit and paint over the sugarpaste to intensify the colour of the rocks and give them a more realistic appearance. Then take a dry stippling brush and stipple over the painted surface to remove the brushstrokes and give a mottled effect. Add a darker colour to the rock recesses to exaggerate their depth, and stipple on some black and white patches to the top of the rocks (**D**). Leave to dry.

Making the mermaid

Creating the tail

1 Roll the sea green modelling paste into a sausage, then taper it to a rounded point and cut to a length of 15cm (6in). Place the tail in position on the cake but do not stick.

2 Indent the top of the tail, where the body will go lightly with your thumb to flatten. Place the indented tail in the palm of your hand and taking the largest piping tube and holding it at 45° press half circles around the top of the body indentation. Add a couple more layers under the first then change to a slightly smaller tube and repeat. Continue reducing the tube size at intervals until you reach the end of the tail. Cut the end of the tail in two with scissors.

3 Roll out the remaining paste between narrow spacers and cut out the tail fin using a cutting wheel. Texture the fin by repeatedly rolling the cutting wheel over the paste, being careful not to cut all the way through (**E**). Place between the two halves of the cut tail section and sugar-glue in place. Lightly dust over the tail with blue and green lustre dusts. Attach the tail in position on the cake.

Making the torso

1 Take a large ball of flesh-coloured modelling paste and roll it into a sausage of a suitable width.

2 Take a palette knife and cut away the bottom of the torso, where it will attach to the tail. Insert a sugar stick or a length of dried spaghetti through the body to help support the head, and place in position on the tail.

Modelling the face

1 Knead some flesh-coloured modelling paste to warm it, then roll into a 2.5cm (1in) ball. Holding a cutter at 45 degrees, indent a mouth (**F**). Make the corners of the mouth by using a small circle cutter, piping tube or cocktail stick (toothpick).

2 Indent eyes with a cocktail stick and add a small ball of paste for a nose. Leave to dry thoroughly before adding small balls of black paste for the eyes. Lightly dust over the cheeks with pink lustre dusts.

Assembling the mermaid

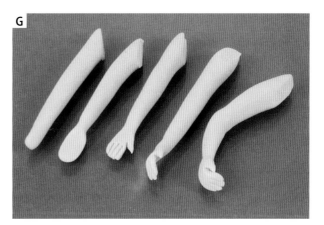

1 Roll a small pea sized ball of flesh modelling paste and stick to the top of the body. Place the head on top.

2 Using the shell mould, create modelling paste shells of the same size and attach to the mermaid's chest using sugar glue. Place a green dragée in between the shells and one at either side. Glue pale green dragées around the joing between the tail and the torso and at the tip of the tail.

Making the arms

1 Roll a tapered sausage of flesh-coloured modelling paste in a suitable size. Roll and thin the paste to shape the wrist. Flatten the hand and, with a pair of small scissors, cut out a small triangle to form the thumb. Roll and thin the paste to form the elbow (**G**).

2 Cut the arms to the required length, ensuring that the hand is in the correct position before making the angular cut. Stick in place.

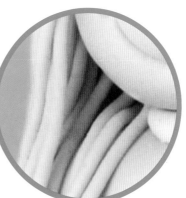

Creating the hair

1 Knead the golden-brown modelling paste until warm then add some white vegetable fat, to stop it getting sticky, and some boiled water to soften the paste. Keep adding a combination of white vegetable fat and boiled water until the paste has the consistency of chewing gum. Place the softened paste in the sugar shaper with the mesh disc. Paint sugar glue over the top of the mermaid's head.

2 Squeeze out a length of hair, remove it from the shaper with a Dresden tool and attach to the back of the head. Continue adding more hair until the head is completely covered.

tip

Why not make some sugar shells for the rock, to make it look more realistic?

Buried Treasure

All pirates have a treasure chest somewhere, and this one is full of hidden gems. It is so simple to create by simply carving your cake to shape, covering with sugarpaste and adding texture and colour for realistic effect. By placing the chest on a wavy blue board and sprinkling light brown sugar around it, you can create your very own treasure island for your friends to discover.

Perfect for a pirate themed birthday party, this cake would really appeal to the imaginations of young children. Why not elaborate on the pirate theme by creating your very own treasure hunt party game? Give the children a map that will lead to the buried treasure – guaranteed to be loved by all.

Fill the chest with your favourite sweet treats and sparkling gems for your little pirates to truly treasure.

you will need ...

materials

- sugarpaste (rolled fondant): white, light brown
- paste colours: selection of blues, brown
- chocolate cake baked in a 7.5 x 12.5cm (3 x 5in) rectangular tin
- modelling paste: gold
- chocolate buttercream
- light brown sugar
- selection of sweets and pearls
- sugar glue

equipment

- 25 x 20cm (10 x 8in) oval cake board
- 15 x 20cm (6 x 8in) cake board cut to shape with a jigsaw
- 7.5 x 12.5cm (3 x 5in) hardboard cake board, cut to fit the cake as necessary.
- cutting wheel
- craft knife
- straight edge, such as a ruler
- large-headed paintbrush

Preparing the board

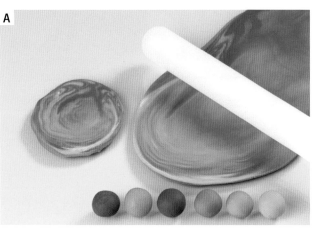

A

1 Take 400g (14oz) of white sugarpaste and colour it in several of shades of blue. Roughly knead these colours together then cut the paste in half to reveal the resulting marbled pattern (**A**).

2 Place the two halves next to each other, cut-side uppermost, and carefully rub the join closed. Roll out the paste, giving it an uneven edge and use to cover the board. Trim, then leave to dry.

tip

When colouring the blue paste, save time by mixing three different blues, then taking small portions of each end kneading them together to create a range of blues that blend.

Preparing the cake

1 Level a rectangular cake (see pages 12–14). Cut a horizontal slice about three quarters of the way up to form the lid. Carve the lid into shape, by curving the top edges using a knife. Place the lid onto the 7.5 x 12.5cm (3 x 5in) cake board.

2 Place the cakes on waxed paper. Spread a thin layer of buttercream over the two cakes. Roll out some light-brown sugarpaste and cover the top of the base. Then for the sides, roll out the sugarpaste, cut one side straight and place on one end of the chest with the straight edge flush with the base. Cut the paste flush with the sides of the chest. Repeat for the other sides of the cake and lid. The paste should be trimmed at the top of the base cake to overlap by 1cm (³⁄₈in), in order to form an indented area to fill with sweets. Leave to dry.

Finishing touches

1 With a straight edge, indent the surface of the paste with lines 1cm (³⁄₈in) apart. Dilute some brown paste colour with clear spirit and paint the chest using a large-headed paintbrush. Leave to dry.

2 Fill the top of the base cake with sweets (candies), pearls and other edible treasures, then attach the lid to the base using sugar glue.

3 Use a craft knife or cutter to cut out a lock shape from gold modelling paste and emboss with your chosen design. Cut out a keyhole using a craft knife and attach roll a small piece of modelling paste to form a knob. Cut the lock shape in half and attach to the top and bottom of the cake, as shown.

4 Place the base on the prepared board and sprinkle light brown sugar around the base to form a sandy island. Add more sweets if desired.

tip

Allow yourself time to get the carving right – if the structure of the cake is correct the rest tends to fall into place.

Fairytale Castle

These irresistible cream and pink towers are quick to make, fun to embellish and will truly steal the hearts of your little princesses. The towers are easily created by covering a swiss roll with sugarpaste and embossing a brickwork pattern into the paste. The turrets are covered with layers of hearts to give a beautiful tiled effect and pearlized gold dragées decorate the cakes to add a sparkling finishing touch.

These mini cakes would make a wonderful gift for the little girl who dreams of princesses and fairytale castles. You can also use the cut hearts and dragées to decorate any other cake to impress your loved ones, such as the adorable heart mini cakes on page 125.

This sweet little turret is made by simply covering an ice-cream cone with pink sugarpaste and 'tiling' it with pink and white modelling-paste hearts.

you will need ...

materials

- sugarpaste (rolled fondant): cream, dark pink, pale pink
- Swiss (jelly) roll of a suitable size or stacked mini cakes cooked in multimini pans
- buttercream
- ice cream cones
- pearlized gold sugar balls
- modelling paste: dark pink and light pink
- sugar glue (see page 19)
- royal icing

equipment

- cake board the same size as the diameter of the cake
- stone-wall embosser (FMM)
- craft knife
- heart cutters
- cutting wheel
- craft knife
- straight edge, such as a ruler

Preparing the cakes

1 Cut a swiss roll in half and cover with a thin layer of buttercream. Roll out some cream sugarpaste into a rectangular shape, the height and circumference of your cake. Roll the cake up in the sugarpaste and cut away any excess paste (shown here on a larger cake – **A**). Rub the join closed, and then trim the paste flush with the top of the cake.

2 Use the stone wall embosser to add the brickwork pattern around the tower (shown here on a larger cake – **B**).

3 Using buttercream stick cake boards to one end of each cake. Stand the cakes upright on their boards. Then add a disc of sugarpaste to the top of each cake.

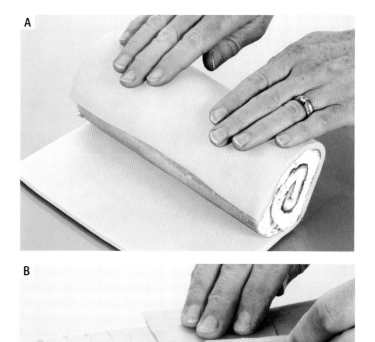

A

B

Decorating the cakes

1 Cut out a window from dark pink sugarpaste. Attach to the middle of the tower using sugar glue and decorate with pearlized gold dragées.

2 To make the turret, cover a large ice-cream cone with pink sugarpaste. Attach to the tower with royal icing. Tile the tower with pink and white modelling-paste hearts. Alternate the pattern of hearts so that some are facing upwards and others downwards and vary the colours to create a layered effect.

3 Roll a small ball of pink sugarpaste and attach to the top of the turret. Decorate around the layers of hearts and bottom of the tower using pearlized gold dragées.

From the heart

Use your little hearts and gold dragees to embellish these stunning little heart-shaped cakes to impress your loved ones. Bake heart-shaped mini and bitesized cakes using the Heart Mini cake and Petite Heart Pans (W) or the multimini heart pan, following instructions on pages 12–14. Cover the cakes with buttercream and then deep-purple sugarpaste. Decorate the cakes with rows of hearts cut from red modelling paste, cut in half and attached along a light pink sugarpaste border line. Add gold dragées between each heart to give the cakes a little sparkle.

Suppliers

UK

Lindy's Cakes Ltd (LC)
Unit 2
Station Approach
Wendover
Bucks
HP22 6BN
Tel: +44 (0)1296 622418
www.lindyscakes.co.uk
*Manufacturer of cutters plus online
shop for equipment used in this and
Lindy's other books*

Knightbridge PME Ltd (W)
Chadwell Heath Lane
Romford
Essex
RN6 4NP
Tel: +44 (0)20 8590 5959
www.cakedecoration.co.uk
UK distributor of Wilton products

M&B Specialised Confectioners Ltd
3a Millmead Estate
Mill Mead road
London
N17 9ND
Tel: +44 (0)20 8801 7948
www.mbsc.co.uk
Manufacturers and suppliers of sugarpaste

US

Global Sugar Art, LLC
625 Route 3
Unit 3
Plattsburgh
NY 12901
Tel: 518 561 3039
www.globalsugarart.com
*Sugarcraft supplier that imports
many UK products to the US*

Wilton Industries, Inc. (W)
2240 West 75th Street
Woodridge
1L 60517
United States
Tel (Retail Customer orders):
+1 800 794 5866
www.wilton.com

Australia

Iced Affair
53 Church Street
Camperdown
NSW 2050
Tel: (02) 9519 3679
www.icedaffair.com.au
Sugarcraft supplier

Abbreviations used in the book:

EA	Edable Art	LC	Lindy's Cakes Ltd
GI	Great Impressions	PME	PME Sugarcraft
FMM	FMM Sugarcraft	SF	Sugarflair
HP	Holly Products	SK	Squire's Kitchen
JEM	Jem Cutters c.c.	W	Wilton

About the Author

Well known, and highly respected in the Sugarcraft industry, Lindy Smith has over 20 years experience in sugarcrafting. Lindy is a designer, who likes to share her love of sugarcraft and inspire fellow enthusiasts by writing books and teaching. Lindy is the author of seven cake decorating titles for D&C: *Creative Celebration Cakes, Storybook Cakes, Celebrate with a Cake!, Party Animal Cakes, Cakes to Inspire and Desire, Bake Me I'm Yours... Cookie* and *Bake Me I'm Yours... Cupcake.*

Lindy's teaching takes her all around the world, giving her the opportunity to educate and inspire whilst also learning about local traditions and cake decorating issues. This knowledge is ultimately then fed back into her work. She has also appeared on television in programmes such as *The Generation Game* and presented a sugarcraft series on *Good Food Live.*

Lindy also heads Lindy's Cakes Ltd, a well-established business that runs her online shop www.lindyscakes.co.uk, and her cake decorating workshops both in the UK and abroad. To see what Lindy is currently doing, become a fan of Lindy's Cakes on Facebook or follow Lindy on Twitter. For baking advice and a wealth of information visit her blog, via the Lindy's Cakes website: www.lindyscakes.co.uk.